The Search for the Codex Cardona

For Pat Lyon

Best Regards

Arnold Bauer

THE SEARCH FOR THE

Codex Cardona

ON THE TRAIL OF A SIXTEENTH-CENTURY MEXICAN TREASURE

Arnold J. Bauer

DUKE UNIVERSITY PRESS   Durham and London 2009

© 2009 Duke University Press
All rights reserved

Printed in the
United States of America
on acid-free paper ⊚

Designed by Jennifer Hill
Typeset in Quadraat by
Tseng Information Systems, Inc.

Library of Congress Cataloging-in-Publication Data
appear on the last printed page of this book.

For
David and Elaine
and
"Alex"

CONTENTS

The search for the Codex Cardona is a true story, grounded in fact and based on interviews, letters, telephone conversations, and e-mail exchanges. I am mindful that human memory is unstable and almost nothing we are told remains the same when retold. Except for three people whose identities I believe prudent to conceal, I use the real names of the experts who wrote learned evaluations of the Codex, the names of the book dealers, museum curators, friends, relatives, and colleagues who enter into the narrative.

On the rare occasions where I did not participate in a conversation or setting that figures in the book, I present the context based on informed imagination and my knowledge of the setting. These infrequent moments are pointed out as such and should be obvious to the reader. The speculation about who might have produced or owned a falsified Codex Cardona is just that: speculation.

ACKNOWLEDGMENTS

 I gratefully acknowledge the cooperation of the people who submitted to my queries and interviews, and I want to express my thanks to a long list of friends and relatives who listened, usually patiently, as I bored on during dinner parties and interminable afternoon coffees about the early stages of this story. Danielle Greenwood, Rebecca Bauer and Quentin Jennings, Kathy Polkinghorn, Richard Schwab, Jo Burr and Ted Margadant, Nancy and Don Price, Dick Curley and Nancy Bramberg, Gloria and Edward Neumeier, Benjamin Orlove, William Farnan, Louis Segal, Gerald and María Elena Foucher, and Carlos Hurtado Ruiz-Tagle were particularly enthusiastic and helpful.

I want to express my profound gratitude to two particularly valuable companions in this project, my dear colleague Charles Walker, who read several drafts of the work, offering wise counsel—saving me from myself—and Andrés Reséndez, who read the drafts, led me to useful sources and people, and accompanied me on an unforgettable day in Mexico City.

Above all, without the persistence, acute judgment, and relentless support of Valerie Millholland, senior editor at Duke University Press, this book would not have been published. A list of conversations, e-mails, and other personal communications appears in the bibliography.

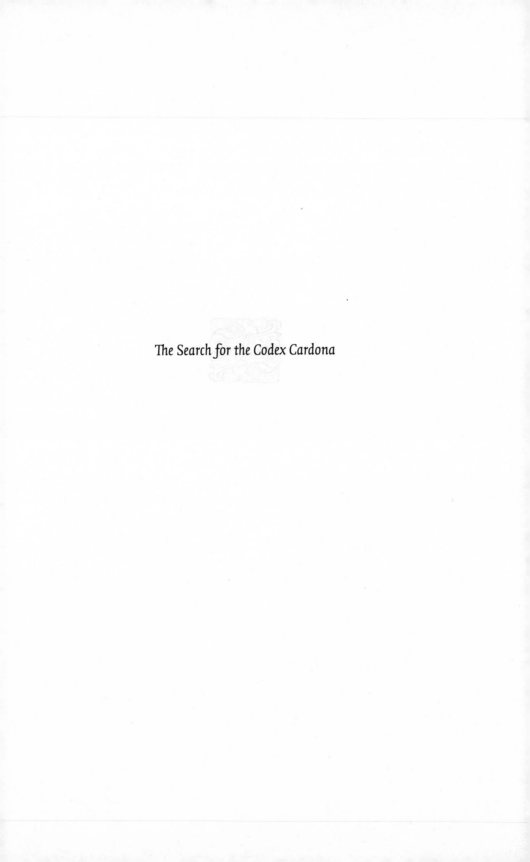

The Search for the Codex Cardona

CHAPTER ONE

The Crocker Lab

Then felt I like some watcher of the skies
When a new planet swims into his ken

JOHN KEATS,
"On First Looking into Chapman's Homer"

 From the outside that afternoon, the Crocker Laboratory looked like a huge, windowless concrete oven, but inside it was cool. Three men bent over a steel bench on which the item we had come to see was opened out. They were an-thropologists and linguists from Stanford University, specialists in pre-Columbian and colonial Mexico. Close by in the air-conditioned lab stood a gentleman wearing dark, baggy pants, a rumpled shirt, and a loosened, gaudy tie. An empty fiber box was propped up against the wall.

Richard Schwab introduced me to Mr. Schwarz—Thomas F. Schwarz—a rare book and manuscript dealer: "Mr. Schwarz, this is my colleague; I hope it's all right with you if he has a peek as well."

Schwarz offered a soft handshake and a glancing, furtive look. As he hovered and darted among the three professors, they carefully turned the oversized pages with the help of a broad wooden paddle, pausing to exam-ine details through a hand-held magnifying glass. What they had before them was an ancient Mexican "painted book," described by Schwarz as the "Codex Cardona." I stepped back from the table. Surprise was an inade-quate term; I was astonished. Schwarz pointed out that there were "four hundred and twenty-seven pages, over three hundred painted illustrations, and two extraordinary maps." These he unfolded from a package inside the hard pasteboard cover of the codex and set them aside.

No one in the room, not even the specialists, had ever heard of a book called the Codex Cardona. There was no mention of this cultural treasure in any of the voluminous literature on early Mexico. The Stanford professors had searched catalogs, archives, and library holdings in Mexico, the United States, and Europe. Incredibly, this remarkable sixteenth-century manuscript seemed to have entered the modern world, brought to the Crocker Laboratory by Thomas Schwarz, in a fiber box tied with canvas straps. But, as we shall see, and what I didn't know then, the Codex Cardona came with lots of baggage that no one knew about on that summer day.

There are several pre-Hispanic and early colonial documents and codices, including jewels such as the Telleriano-Remensis and the Codex Mendoza now held in Paris and Oxford, and fragments of other rare pre-Columbian and postconquest documents in libraries and museums in Rome, Florence, Mexico City, and the Vatican, to name a few. But the Codex Cardona, with many more pages than any of these and hundreds of illustrations, not to mention the oversized, foldout maps, was truly dazzling. As Schwarz carefully leafed through the pages, which crackled a bit to the touch, the Stanford professors spoke to each other quietly, pointing out this and that detail.

In part similar to the *Tira de la peregrinación*, of which I'd seen a reproduction in Mexico's grand Museum of Anthropology and History several years ago, the Codex Cardona began by tracking the chronology of the Mexica—or Nahuas—from their hazy twelfth-century beginnings to the founding of Tenochtitlán a hundred years later. According to a typewritten inventory that Schwarz handed around, the codex then dealt with the catastrophic conquest by the Spaniards from 1519 to 1521, continuing with sketches, text, and paintings of early Mexico, down to the time the codex was actually produced—or said to have been produced—between 1550 and 1556. The scribes and painters worked under the direction of one Captain Alonzo Cardona y Villaviciosa, a crown official, whose own orders had come directly from the first viceroy of Mexico, don Antonio de Mendoza.

The Mexica or Nahuas—commonly known since the eighteenth century as the Aztecs—settled in the high intermontane Valley of Mexico in the early fourteenth century and still occupied a large swathe of it in the years after the Spanish conquest. Their descendants, of course, still live there today, a good part of one of the planet's largest cities. The painted illustrations in the Codex Cardona were accompanied by explanatory text, written, perhaps by Catholic clergy—Franciscans and Dominicans most likely—in the nearly indecipherable sixteenth-century script that to the layperson looks as much like Arabic as Spanish.

As Schwarz patiently lifted the pages, one could see that on nearly every one, native artists had traced with quill and brush, in still-vivid blue, vermillion, and green paint, and rust-colored and black inks, the details of daily life and descriptions of flora and fauna. The pictures showed tools and plants, birds and feathers, gods and sacrifice, the ways of farming and irrigation, family life, and women's dress. Several drawings of corpses in cotton shrouds offered confirmation of the widespread death caused by the European invaders' deadly pathogens. There was one page, touching in its simplicity, showing the conqueror, Hernán Cortés himself, carrying one corner of his deceased wife's coffin. Three or four folios showed two different native women seated in European chairs. One was described as having written a native account of the conquest, another as having gathered weapons for an uprising, frustrated by the Spanish occupiers and severely repressed.

I felt like an outsider to Schwarz's presentation, but he didn't seem to mind my uninvited presence. The Stanford professors, absorbed in the show, didn't seem to notice my presence, or perhaps thought it bad manners to object. Schwab stayed discreetly back while I had a good look at several pages and illustrations. When I expressed admiration, Schwarz, to my utter astonishment, reached over the Codex, tore a fingernail-sized piece off the corner of one folio, and handed it to me. Stunned, I put it in my pocket.

Finally Schwarz produced the maps, two double foldout elephant folios. One was a rust-colored street-by-street map of the great lacustrine metropolis of Tenochtitlán just then being rebuilt as Mexico City; another showed the streets and named the first Spanish settlers of the now elegant suburb of Coyoacán.

"A treasure of incalculable value in itself," Schwarz pointed out, referring to the Tenochtitlán map.

"There's nothing like it," one of the professors said, nodding to his colleague, "except for the Santa Cruz one in Uppsala."

It was hard not to be enthralled by the presence of the codex; yet the overall feeling that arose from those exotic pages as I watched Schwarz leaf through the book was a kind of inescapable melancholy or resignation, as if the native artists, working under the orders of Captain Cardona, had projected backward into the chronicle the gloom of their recent defeat. Or maybe the Aztecs' own ineluctable sense of tragedy was itself the cause of their demise.

In any case, the Stanford anthropologists were undoubtedly persuaded not only that the Codex Cardona would alter the ethnohistory of early Mexico but that its presence at Stanford would translate into grants and more graduate students, international conferences, new careers, not to mention a large publicity splash. The Codex Cardona, brought into public view centuries after being created, would make the brilliant centerpiece in an already imposing collection of rare books and incunabula. Such treasures, they must have thought, came along once in a lifetime. From what I'd seen, it was almost as if the Aztec illustrators had drawn up this spectacular document to describe those distant years when their own world was fast disappearing and a new one being built, sealed the roll of pages in a huge bottle, and tossed it into the sea. Now, nearly four and a half centuries later, it had washed up on a distant shore. On exactly whose shore, Mr. Schwarz was not telling.

The Crocker Laboratory had agreed to examine the Codex Cardona by means of PIXE (particle-induced x-ray emission) analyses of its paper and ink to determine whether the codex was an authentic mid-sixteenth-century work, a later copy, or an elaborate fraud produced after 1945, as one radiocarbon test suggested. An unnamed owner was offering the codex for sale to Stanford University's Special Collections Library for between six and seven million dollars. Doubts, however, had been raised about the book's authenticity and, consequently, about its provenance.

My colleague Richard Schwab, the man who introduced me to the Codex Cardona, was a historical sleuth who had spent the better part of a diligent career tracking down pirated and fraudulent versions of the eighteenth-century French Encyclopédie, about which he wrote articles in obscure scholarly journals.

A few years ago, a University of California physicist had developed a method for evaluating the makeup of inks and dyes in old documents and comparing them with others of known provenance to determine their authenticity, and he had enlisted Schwab's historical expertise to complement the process. This appealed to my friend's subversive nature and renewed his interest in history.

Schwab and his physicist colleague carried out their examinations without manhandling or clipping off pieces of the items they examined. Their technique, in addition to being noninvasive and high-tech, added a new dimension to conventional dating techniques. Libraries and book dealers brought copies of the Gutenberg Bible to the Crocker Laboratory, and there was talk about having a shot at the Shroud of Turin. They had also gotten immersed in the flap over the so-called Vinland map, ending up on the wrong side of an intense debate about the titanium content in the ink.[1] It turned out that the map, sold to Yale University in 1964 as a genuine fifteenth-century artifact, had in fact been drawn with ink manufactured after 1923. Nevertheless the Crocker Lab's reputation for other work, discussed in scientific journals as well as in *Time* magazine, remained intact, so that buyers for universities' special collections departments and prestigious museums, more wary than ever of fraud and forgers after the Vinland map scandal, had little hesitation in paying for the lab's services.

By the time we left the cool concrete-and-steel lab, the wind had dropped off, and a flat, dead heat pressed against the earth. I was knocked out by what I'd seen.

"It's really fascinating, don't you think?" Schwab said in his conspiratorial tone. "It's spectacular. I never knew the Aztecs were so pornographic."

I hadn't seen any evidence of that, and I wondered what he meant.

"Do you think the lab will be able to tell if it's the real thing?" I asked.

"It's hard to know. We can say something about the makeup of the inks and paints, but any forger worth his salt would figure out a way to make them the way they did back then. We'd really need samples from other documents, contemporary with the Cardona, to compare the inks and paint. Did you understand that there's a rather dubious radiocarbon date suggesting a post-1945 origin?"

We stopped under a row of cork trees.

"Look, I've got to go. Thanks for asking me along; if you hadn't, this thing would have just come and gone, and I'd never have seen it."

I was off to meet Alexandra (Alex), my new love, at the nursery; she wanted to pick up two Cécile Brunners for the trellis.

"I'll let you know what happens," Schwab said. "I think Schwarz is taking the book back down to Stanford tomorrow."

I woke early the next day and went to the university library to begin researching Mexican codices. In a never-ending search for new projects, I had already begun to think that I might write something about the Codex Cardona and the dramatic world it described: the surprise appearance in

Easter week of 1519 of 510 Spaniards—only twelve on horseback—among the hundreds of thousands of people in the most astonishing native kingdom in the Western Hemisphere; the invaders' capture of the emperor Moctezuma; the consequent fierce uprising of the Aztecs followed by the Spanish-led siege that brought death and destruction to the resplendent island capital; and later the rebuilding of a late medieval Christian city and society on the ruins.

This picture is what the nameless illustrators of the Codex Cardona seemed determined to capture: a panoramic snapshot of a long moment in time showing the persistence of an ancient culture amid the bewildering chaos of the new. There is more than one gripping written account of these years, but nowhere that I knew was there a book of three hundred painted illustrations and detailed maps that provides such a touching, rustic, and authentic picture of daily life in these decades of the first encounter between Europe and America.

I didn't have a professional knowledge of Mexican codices, but maybe, I thought, I could do something different from my usual academic scribbling. Treat the Codex Cardona as a mystery, perhaps? After all, it had disappeared 450 years ago and then, inexplicably, came to be laid out on a steel table in California. Or if the Crocker Lab finds it really *isn't* authentic, better yet! Who could possibly have forged it? Maybe I could imagine an ingenious falsifier. Or I could simply tell the Cardona's story: try my hand at the kind of investigative journalism you see in the *New Yorker*, to find out where it came from, how it was acquired? Such a story could be anchored in fact—not "fact" in quotation marks, as most of my colleagues now wrote— it could be a *true* story, something I'm more comfortable with. Anyway, the whole thing was certainly worth a try, and a surgical strike on the university library's Mesoamerican collection was the place to start.

The library has aisles and aisles of books, large volumes of handsome reproductions of codices, collections of documents, lots of Mexican archaeology and paleoanthropology and history in Special Collections and in the stacks. I held in my hands a beautiful edition, published by a Mexican bank, of Lord Kingsborough's multivolume reproductions of the *Antiguedades de México*; the recent definitive four-volume work on the famous Codex Mendoza, and numerous other facsimiles by French and German scholars. I perused the indispensable *Handbook of Middle American Indians* in several volumes; studies by the Englishman Gordon Brotherston, the American H. B. Nicholson, the great Mexicans Alfonso Caso and Miguel León-Portilla, the

Frenchman Jacques Soustelle; and stories of spectacular discoveries, to name just a small part of the literature. My first reconnaissance revealed no mention anywhere of a Codex Cardona or of any Captain Cardona under whose immediate direction the book was supposed to have been created. I scanned through the *Catálogo de pasajeros a Indias*, an exhaustive list of Spaniards who had gone out to the New World in the sixteenth century. No Cardona y Villaviciosa.

Turning to the general subject of native documents, the first thing I learned was that of all the Native Americans from Hudson Bay to Patagonia, only the people in Mesoamerica (present-day central Mexico and Guatemala) created what the Aztecs called *amoxtli* and the Maya *tataah*. The first Spaniards to arrive in Mexico knew these artifacts as *libros de pintura*, or painted books, and by the eighteenth century they came to be known by the ancient European term *codex*. Their history in Mesoamerica dates back to the classic period (ca. 300–900 A.D.), and by the time of the Spanish invasion, codices in a wide variety of forms could be found everywhere, particularly in the Nahuatl-speaking region centered on Mexico-Tenochtitlán and among the Mixtec of Oaxaca.

Hundreds, perhaps thousands, of specialized *tlahcuilos* (scribe-painters) did their work in the *tlahcuiloyan* (a place for writing and painting roughly analogous to the medieval scriptorium), producing records of tribal origins, noble lineages, accounts of wars and tax collection, descriptions of ritual, almanacs, and the commercial accounts of long-distance traders.[2]

To record this information, the Aztecs required stacks and stacks of amate paper, made from a variety of New World fig trees (genus *Ficus*) and other plants, as tribute from their subjects. One Indian community alone, in the Sierra of Puebla northeast of Tenochtitlán, came up with "ocho mil pliegos de papel de la tierra" (eight thousand sheets of locally made paper) every year.[3] But of all the "painted books" compiled by native scribes and painters before the arrival of the Europeans, only a dozen—none of them from Mexico-Tenochtitlán—survived the Spanish conquest.

Reading through the accounts in the library, I could easily see that the Spanish invaders in the early sixteenth century were at least as zealous as our present-day fundamentalists and equally intolerant. They brought with them what they believed was the "true faith," a religious ideology forged in the conflict with Islam in the fifteenth-century Mediterranean and then made all the more inflexible by the Protestant assault in the homeland of European Catholicism itself. At almost the same time that Luther was nailing his *Ninety-five Theses* to the church door in Wittenberg, Hernán Cortés was carrying the banner of the True Cross—la Vera Cruz—ashore at the port named for it on Mexico's gulf coast. At the same time, several of the early friars sent to evangelize among the Aztecs had previously participated in the conquest of Granada from the Moors and the expulsion of the Jews from Spain in 1492, and they carried their messianic zeal to Mexico.

The conquistadors, and particularly the friars who accompanied the expeditions, alarmed by the exotic warriors and lightning-bolt deities depicted in many of the painted books, naturally associated the codices with the local religion they were determined to eradicate. The Spanish intruders were quick to see the devil's hand in the brilliantly colored, elaborate glyphs and pictorial writing. Impatient to bring the native people into the Christian fold, they undertook a process called the "spiritual conquest" (and, when resisted, the "extirpation of idolatry"), so that even the clergy most interested in native culture—humanist friars such as Diego de Landa in the Yucatán or Zumárraga or Sahagún in Mexico—urged on the bonfires whose flames devoured uncounted piles of manuscripts. In a further irony, today the few surviving native codices are named not for those who painted or wrote them but for the place, usually in Europe, where they are currently held. These include the Codex Vaticano II, the Florentine Codex, the Dresden, Borgia, and Vindobonense—names that no doubt would seem peculiar to the original artists were they alive today.

For the next several weeks, I went back to the university library and got other books through interlibrary loan. The making of painted books did not end with the Spanish conquest of Mexico. Native tlahcuiloyan continued to turn out a stream of documents and books. Working clandestinely, some tried to keep alive the memory of their vanishing culture; others worked under the interested and watchful eyes of the remarkable generation of postconquest humanist Spanish friars. The painted books that continued to depict proscribed material were destroyed when found, their patrons and painters hauled before the Spanish authorities. At the same time, inquisitive Spanish officials commissioned native scribes to create other codices, useful to the invaders for understanding local culture and economy.

Consequently, in the generations following the conquest, native artists working under Spanish direction produced a good many elaborately painted books; some five hundred colonial indigenous documents are presently known. They range from a single page or even a single illustration to several folded sheets of deerskin or *amate* to spectacular books treasured by prestigious libraries in Europe and the United States. The best of the originals were usually on European paper available in the Atlantic trade.

The Codex Cardona, then, *if* authentic, belongs to this postconquest body of work. It's all the more intriguing, however, because its three hundred illustrations, two large exceptional maps, and 427 pages of text and illustration in all would make it the most extensive single Mexican codex. Even more astonishing, the Cardona did not appear publicly for over four hundred years after it was presumably made. It still has no public record, even in the most recent scholarship.

CHAPTER TWO

A World of Painted Books

He showed it to me and told me that he had made it . . . that it set
down information about the land since the founding of this city of
México, and about the lords that had governed and ruled until
the coming of the Spaniards.

NICHOLSON, "History of the Codex Mendoza"

 But was the Codex Cardona authentic? If so, where did it
come from? Had it really been drawn up and painted in the
mid-sixteenth century and then tucked away somewhere all
this time? Who was its present owner? Wasn't its sale across
international borders governed by laws of cultural patrimony?

Even a casual reader of newspapers and journals knows that the arena of
old documents, paintings, antiquities, and rare book dealers is a fascinating
place, a world in itself, made glamorous by big money and peopled with brilliant and cultivated experts, scoundrels, fakers, and frauds, even criminals.
Mr. Schwarz had offered to sell the Codex Cardona to Stanford University
for between six and seven million dollars. His client, whose name he "was
not at liberty to divulge," was at first casually described as "a gentleman of
Hispanic descent resident in London" and at another time, also vaguely, as
an Englishman who had acquired the codex from a "Spanish family."

In fact, Mr. Schwarz had been given no documentation, no proof of
ownership at all. Greed and doubt are often present in the antiquities trade,
but Schwarz's casual appearance, his anonymous client, and the document's long disappearance didn't help to allay doubts.

Attached to the inside lid of the Cardona's fiber case was a packet of
letters, test results, reports, and scholarly opinions from a number of specialists. The Stanford professors had presumably seen this material, but it

wasn't handed to me that day in the Crocker Lab; and, of course, it wouldn't have been appropriate to ask for it. The experts, Schwarz emphasized, agreed that in every detail the names, dates, acts, and events recorded in the Codex Cardona squared with present knowledge about sixteenth-century Mexico. Illustrations in several of the folios showed construction in the years 1554–56 of a massive dike, the albarradón, designed to prevent salt water from entering the Chalco Lake. There are only scattered references to the dike in modern scholarship, but several of the painted and detailed illustrations were devoted to the albarradón. One showed pairs of women in a shallow launch, patting out and cooking over a *comal* (griddle) the eternal corn tortilla, a staple of Indian diet for millennia, here even in the middle of a lake. The codex shows on the margin of one of its maps the archaeological detail of a partly buried mid-sixteenth-century primitive church in a dig opened in 1982 by the construction of the Zócalo metro station in the center of colonial Mexico City. One specialist who provided an opinion on the codex believes this shows the authenticity of the Codex Cardona, because a forger working in, say, the 1940s could not have known of a building that only came to light in 1982. However, knowledge of a mid-sixteenth-century church, which was subsequently buried in the sinking soil of Mexico City and then *re*-appeared after 1980, would also have been available to a historically informed forger.

The hundreds of pictographs bore comparison with the style of other contemporary mid-sixteenth-century Mexican codices. The ethnographic detail of the neighboring city of Tlatelolco agreed with the research of modern scholars; in fact, the codex presents hitherto unknown information on the Franciscan friars who had established their legendary *colegio* for the native elite in Tlatelolco on what is now the Plaza of the Three Cultures. If the Cardona was a modern forgery, clearly it was an extraordinarily laborious and informed—and indeed a brilliant—work.

Against some persistent doubts, such as those about the kind of paper and ink used in the codex, Schwarz had emphasized to the Stanford professors the overwhelming weight of positive evidence. Nothing in the codex's voluminous detail was contradicted by current scholarship; the illustrations seemed unquestionably the work of native painters, and the specialists agreed that the Spanish annotations seemed to be in the sixteenth-century hand. Forgery seemed as unimaginable to the experts asked to evaluate the work as it did to the Stanford anthropologists gathered in the Crocker Lab.

Moreover, how could a team of exquisitely trained forgers have been assembled? And if they had existed, who was the driven genius that had directed them?

While Schwarz held forth that afternoon, I silently ran over in my head a few names I was familiar with. Could the forger have been Dr. Miguel León-Portilla, the dean of Nahuatl studies at the National Autonomous University of Mexico and a man of undoubted and even pious probity? One of the keen and impoverished Mexican teachers from the 1930s, when *indigenismo* and Mexican antiquities were all the rage? A foreign scholar such as the brilliant Jacques Soustelle or the American James Lockhart with his coterie of Nahuatl students? Impossible to imagine! But then, if the codex *were* authentic, how could such a document, created in the mid-sixteenth century, lie unnoticed for over four hundred years? And above all, why the secrecy? Why did Schwarz's mysterious client in London not call a press conference to announce his prize? International publicity, after all, would only have driven the price higher.

At the same time, any rare book and manuscript dealer — or the codex's owner — would have to be aware of the clamor, growing louder since the 1970s, for the recovery of cultural treasures hauled away by powerful nations or sold off to rich collectors abroad. The demand for restitution of national artifacts is often inspired by nationalist sentiment. The Greeks have long wanted the Parthenon marbles returned from the British Museum to Athens, the Egyptians want the Rosetta stone from the same institution, and recently the Peruvians have insisted that Yale University return the artifacts taken from Machu Picchu. And dealers and libraries in the United States have increasingly been questioned about holding manuscripts of doubtful provenance.

But then, it's also true that the Cardona is not the first painting or manuscript or even painted book to lie neglected, out of sight for centuries, before being "discovered" in recent times. I thought immediately of a well-known case, closer to my own field of study: the two-volume, nearly twelve-hundred-page illustrated account put together by a native Peruvian, Felipe Guaman Poma de Ayala. This remarkable work, in part a condemnation of Spanish rule in Peru, was presumably carried down from the Peruvian highlands to Lima in the first years of the seventeenth century and presented to the viceroy or to one of his secretaries. There is no record, or at least no one has found a written reaction, of its acceptance in Lima. The book, known as *Nueva corónica* [sic] *y buen gobierno*, was apparently carried by sailing vessel up the west coast of South America, lugged on mule back across the humid and dangerous Isthmus of Panama, shipped by galleon to Seville, and then somehow found its way to Philip IV's powerful minister, Count-Duke Olivares. And then, somehow, to the Danish Royal Library in Copenhagen, where it lay apparently unknown or neglected for perhaps 250 years before being brought to public attention in 1908.

So these things can happen. The Cardona could have lain out of sight, like the Guaman Poma book, say, in a big manorial house in Spain for two centuries, and before that, God knows where. There's no doubt that the Cardona is Mexican; perhaps it lay neglected and ignored in the corner of some colonial monastery in Mexico?

Fabulous things appear out of the blue. In the late 1980s, a dealer offered a sculpture of an unknown Greek goddess, thought to be a representation of Aphrodite, to Ms. Marion True, former curator of antiquities at the J. Paul Getty Museum. The piece had a mysterious background — it had been stored in an empty warehouse in England — and the subsequent battle over provenance involved the Italian culture ministry, criminal dealers, and international police, eventually causing Ms. True to lose her job. The provenance of the statue is still unclear.[1]

So the Cardona had a murky past. But compared with what? It became clear to me while scanning through the accounts of other codices in the library that even the best known and most famous of them had been lost, reappeared, disappeared again, and then showed up in unlikely places. Some of the more valuable ones did not come into public view until the last two centuries.

I remembered discussions in graduate school about other codices, so I took a closer look at the collection of facsimile reproductions in the library and focused particularly on the stories of two well-known early-sixteenth-century Mexican painted books in order to have some sort of perspective on the Cardona's own hard-to-pin-down past. Both of these facsimile editions were published during the past ten years in impressive and expensive reproductions. They are the most famous contemporaries of the Cardona; both are accompanied by expert scholarly analyses.

The first to consider is the Codex Telleriano-Remensis, produced between 1552 and 1563 and consequently almost an exact contemporary of the Cardona. It too has a murky history and was shunted along a halting, hidden path until coming into public view in Paris nearly 250 years after it was created by Nahuatl-speaking artists in a native workshop under Spanish direction in the Aztec capital. Unlike the Cardona, however, the Telleriano-Remensis left a paper trail, so at least its authenticity as a true mid-sixteenth-century codex has not been questioned.

Shorter than the Codex Cardona, the Telleriano-Remensis's fifty folios display, in still bright color, three separate sections: the *xiuhpohualli*, a 365-day solar calendar; the glyphic figures representing deities of the feast days of the *tonalámatl*, the Aztec divinatory almanac of twenty eighteen-day months; and a mythical-historical account, running, in the words of the Spanish gloss, from "the year of 11 reed according to their [i.e., the native] count and the year 1399 according to ours, to the year of 5 rabbit or 1562." This historical or dynastic chronicle depicts warriors, lords, major battles, earthquakes, and comets. We see the famous dedication of the Templo Mayor in Tenochtitlán, which required four thousand human sacrifices; paintings of uprisings against the Spanish occupation; and, as in the Cardona, pictures of stacked corpses, the victims of smallpox and measles.

At least two Christianized native painters and six Spanish scribes carried out the work of painting the Telleriano-Remensis over a period of eleven years. It seems that Dominican and probably Franciscan friars, working closely with translators conversant not only with Nahuatl and Spanish but also with native tradition, were involved in the work. Unlike the Cardona's *amate*, the Telleriano-Remensis is on watermarked European paper.

No written evidence survives, however, about the compilation of the Telleriano-Remensis. Because it was painted by indigenous artists and annotated by at least one scribe who was known to have lived in Mexico, it's safe to assume that the book was produced there. There were two painters, one so highly accomplished that the foremost scholar of this codex believes he was trained by a master painter, possibly in the preconquest period. Of the six scribes, only one can be identified—and little is known about him—an elusive Dominican friar or lay brother named Pedro de los Ríos. The glosses accompanying the paintings are in both Spanish and Nahuatl; the main text is in Spanish.

Nor is it known how the Telleriano-Remensis came into the possession of Charles-Maurice Le Tellier (for whom it is named), the archbishop of Reims and a famous bibliophile, in 1701. The documentation of the codex begins then, and only then, because that year, the archbishop decided to donate the painted book, identified in a Reims catalog as *liber scriptus charac-*

teribus et figuris mexicanis, to the Bibliothèque du Roi—the *roi* being at the time his close friend Louis XIV, the Sun King.

After its transfer to the library of Louis XIV, however, the *liber scriptus* disappeared again for over a century, or at least attracted no recorded interest, until Alexander von Humboldt, that indefatigable explorer and naturalist, returned to Paris from his travels in South America, Mexico, and the United States. Von Humboldt was said to have read nearly all the books in print during his lifetime in German, French, and English (and probably many in other languages). Nevertheless, finding the Telleriano-Remensis while rummaging around the Bibliothèque National in 1804 must have been a pleasant surprise. Since then, at least three reproductions of the Telleriano-Remensis have been made to bring this remarkable document to the attention of scholars who do not have the resources to enjoy long visits to Paris.

Although the Telleriano-Remensis was produced in Mexico during the same decade as the Cardona, it was easy to see that the Telleriano-Remensis contains more indigenous content; that is, it deals more with the pre-Hispanic world than does the Cardona. Nevertheless, the two codices are similar in several ways: both use native glyphs, both take up Aztec foundational myths, and both are the work of Hispanized native painters and Spanish-speaking scribes. The major difference between these two spectacular documents of the first postconquest generation is the scope and detail of the 427-page Cardona compared to the 50 folios of the Telleriano-Remensis. It's also true that the Cardona's illustrations are rustic compared with the high indigenous art of the Telleriano-Remensis.[2]

A second Mexican painted book of the mid-sixteenth century is the Codex Mendoza, about which its principal scholar says, "None of the [colonial codices] is more magnificent or informative."[3] The Mendoza is also a product of the first postconquest generation, and two of its three parts are similar in content to, if better executed than, the Cardona. And like the Telleriano-Remensis, the Mendoza's twisting and discontinuous travels, ending finally in Oxford's Bodleian Library, make a fascinating story in themselves, fraught with drama and adventure.

The Codex Mendoza was produced most likely between 1541 and 1547 and, like the Cardona, at the bidding of Mexico's first viceroy, Antonio de Mendoza, for whom the codex is named. Don Antonio apparently wanted to obtain a firsthand account of Aztec life while the preconquest natives still lived. Keen to acquaint the Spanish monarch Charles V with his new subjects, the viceroy sent off the codex from Vera Cruz on a Spanish galleon bound for Seville. En route, however, a French corsair captured the ship and hauled the booty to the court of Henri II. Someone—it's not known who—then apparently handed the codex over to André Thevet, the king's *cosmographe*.

Somehow, Richard Hakluyt, chaplain to the English ambassador to France, acquired the painted book for only twenty crowns. Sometime after 1616, it was passed on to Samuel Purchas, a compiler of travel books, whose son sold it to John Selden, a collector of New World manuscripts. Five years after Selden died in 1654, the Codex Mendoza entered the Bodleian collection—where it lay forgotten for another 170 years until the eccentric Edward King (Lord Kingsborough) discovered it.

Kingsborough was so impressed with the Mendoza that he featured a reproduction of it in his monumental nine-volume series *Antiquities of Mexico*, published between 1831 and 1848, a work so elaborate and costly that he was driven into debt and died of typhus in a Dublin jail. An excessive price, some might say, for dedication to scholarship.

Kingsborough offered no explanation of the codex's pictographs but rather concentrated on his obsessive quest to prove that the Aztecs were one of the lost tribes of Israel. Nevertheless *Antiquities of Mexico* brought to scholarly life the few then-recognized pre-Hispanic Mexican codices, as well as the Mendoza and the Telleriano-Remensis, Vaticanus A, and several others in all their vivid colors, with glyphs and original texts.

A century later, in 1938, Major James Cooper-Clark brought out a second and even more beautiful reproduction of the Codex Mendoza in three volumes. This edition is scarce because in 1940, during the Blitz, German bombers destroyed almost the entire press run. In 1995 two North American scholars produced a definitive edition of the Mendoza in four volumes, on which I have relied.

The Codex Mendoza, like the Telleriano-Remensis painted on European paper, is made up of three parts. The first depicts in native glyphs and annotated text the historico-mythological sequence of the Aztec conquests up to the founding of their capital of Tenochtitlán.

The second part, thirty-seven folios in all, consists of copies of either pre-Hispanic or immediate postconquest tax rolls, showing the tribute due from the thirty-eight provinces surrounding the imperial capital from 1516 to 1518, just before the Spanish conquest. Glyphs of tributary towns are represented along the left-hand margin, and ideograms indicate the tribute of feathered costumes, fine cloth, jaguar pelts, and live eagles, along with everyday items such as maize, beans, and cacao. These unusual folios paint a graphic picture of the tons of food, thousands of pieces of cotton cloth, hundreds of building beams, and thousands of sheets of *amate* that flowed each year from subject people to Tenochtitlán.

The Mendoza's third part, which comprises fifteen folios, is closest in content to the Cardona except that it provides a snapshot of Mexico *before* the conquest, whereas the Cardona takes up the consequences of reconstruction in the years after the Spanish occupation.

The illustrations in the third section of the Mendoza are devoted to ethnographic detail. They depict the life cycle of the Aztecs, beginning with the ceremonial bathing of the newborn child. A number of severe punishments accompany the passage through childhood, including pricks with cactus thorns and the forced inhalation of burning chili smoke. These measures aimed at imposing obedience, moderation, and diligence. We see how alternate "career paths" were organized and led to training as warriors and priests or in the practical crafts. The Aztecs supported a gendered division of labor in which boys fished and hunted while girls are shown with broom and spindle and, most importantly, bent over the ubiquitous *metate* (mortar), grinding *nixtamal*, the Mexican staff of life for the past four thousand years.

The Codex Cardona, then, belongs to the universe of postconquest Mexican codices and is in some sense a predecessor of the *Relaciones geográficas* of the 1570s and 1580s. The Cardona's illustrations lack the high art of either the Telleriano-Remensis or the Mendoza, perhaps because the native tradition of master painters had begun to fade by the 1550s; but in its ethnographic richness, in the almost gossipy accounts of heretofore unnoticed people, in its architectural detail, in its depictions of agricultural and irrigation practices, and above all in its three hundred illustrations and many stunning maps, the Cardona goes beyond its two principal sister codices of the first postconquest generation.

My excursions into the world of Mexican codices was revealing. In the first place, there was a lot I didn't know about Mexican painted books, and at the same time their very existence had become even more intriguing. The second thing was that a great lot of uncertainty hangs over all the major Mexican codices, not just the Cardona. The circumstances surrounding their preparation and destiny are obscure. This could hardly be otherwise given the tumultuous decades following the Spanish invasion of Mexico, when after two years of the bloody siege of the Aztec capital the invaders ransacked the ruins for the spoils of conquest. The Spaniards were not, of course, an organized or disciplined army but rather a contentious lot of rivals out for the main chance, eager to loot and plunder, to grab property and the rights to exploit the native peasantry. Right behind and even beside the soldiers were the zealous clergy, some dedicated to the harvesting of souls, others keen to understand a strange New World and to spread news of its existence back to their European homeland.

The means to spread the news was the written word. Cortés had barely stepped ashore at Vera Cruz when he asked for pen and ink to write a letter to his sovereign, the Habsburg king of Spain, Charles V. Other reports followed—private letters, official documents from a paper-mad royal and clerical bureaucracy—and soon, in a matter of a decade or two, the crown commissioned multivolume histories to describe the newly found Indies.

If the English gained their empire in a fit of absent-mindedness, the Spanish imperialists were dedicated, purposeful bureaucrats almost from the start. At the same time, colonial officials from the viceroy down—particularly the mendicant clergy, mainly the Franciscans and Dominicans—encouraged the newly conquered people to record their own histories in painted books. The friars, of course, kept a steady gaze over the shoulder of the native painters, asking native translators for assistance and writing explanatory textual annotations in Spanish.

There were many ways that colonial documents, artifacts, and books might go astray in the heady first years of the conquest. A famous example is the artifact known as "Moctezuma's headdress," made of many three-foot-long green feathers taken from the shy quetzal bird, along with beads and precious metals. Aiming to impress the Spanish emperor with the barbaric splendor of his New World realms, someone in Mexico—no one knows who—sent the object to Europe and eventually to Vienna, Charles V's occasional residence, where, in spite of Mexican objection, the headdress is prominently displayed today. No record, however, exists of its passage—no shipping manifest, no receipt. Few believe today that the headdress ever actually belonged to Moctezuma, and in fact, for a long time, conventional opinion held that it was a device or standard. It was Zelia Nuttall, a brilliant and slightly zany anthropologist from San Francisco, whose feminine insight led to identification of the object in the 1880s as most likely a headdress. She not only wrote a learned article for Harvard's Peabody

Museum but dramatized her argument by wearing—one imagines with great panache—a homemade model of the headdress at the International Congress of Americanists in Paris, creating un succès de scandale among her apparently humorless male colleagues.[4]

To grasp some sense of the doubt and confusion about the provenance of early colonial artifacts—an issue that so troubles modern collectors—and why so many native documents and codices could so easily have gone astray between their American origin and European destination, we might, in our mind's eye, imagine the path taken in the early sixteenth century by one of the early codices from Mexico-Tenochtitlán to France.

A good example, again, is the highly visible and officially sponsored Codex Mendoza, whose trajectory, one would think, should have left a paper trail. Although commissioned by Viceroy Mendoza himself, the book's origin is obscure. It is possible that we first glimpse the Codex Mendoza in a Mexico-Tenochtitlán workshop in 1547, when the book would have been near completion. One of the early conquistadors, writing to the viceroy about a matter that had nothing to do with codices, told of a book he had seen:

> It must have been about six years ago more or less, that entering into the house of an Indian who was called Gualpoyogualcal, master of painters, I saw in his possession a book with covers of parchment. Asking him what it was, in secret he showed it to me and told me that he had made it by command of Your Lordship and in which he set down information about the land since the founding of this city of Mexico and the lords that had governed and ruled until the coming of the Spaniards . . . and the assignment of these towns and provinces that was made by Moctezuma to the principal lords of this city and the fees that . . . each one gave him from the tributes of the towns . . . and how he sketched the towns and provinces for it.[5]

Some scholars believe this may have been the Codex Mendoza, and perhaps it was; but there were several such books "with covers of parchment" containing tribute lists and maps along with descriptions "of towns and provinces" knocking about in early colonial Mexico, almost all of them now lost. Six years earlier the viceroy himself had written in a letter dated October 6, 1541, that he was preparing a "relación of the things of this land." Was this the painted book that came to be known as the Codex Mendoza? It's hard to know. It could just as well have been another *relación* — since there were many — maybe even the Codex Cardona.

In any case, once a codex such as the Mendoza had been finished, wrapped, and sealed, it would have been placed in a specially constructed waterproof box, wrapped tightly in oilcloth, and loaded into a leather bag lashed to a mule's flank. The only alternative to mules — they had been introduced to America only twenty years earlier but had multiplied like mad — was human carriers. In fact, that was the only way of moving goods in pre-Cortesian Mexico, since there were no wheelbarrows or carts, and the Andean llamas had not found their way north of Panama (nor have they today, in any numbers). Whether by human carrier or mule back, the journey from the high valley of Mexico down to the coast followed footpaths over nine-thousand-foot mountain passes, down the steep escarpment of the Sierra Madre Oriental to the humid, rainy, pestilential port of Vera Cruz. There cargo might remain for weeks, even months, before being lightered out through the surf to a storm-battered caravel or galleon bobbing in the waters of the Gulf.

The ship waited for fair weather to beat out against the Trades through the passage between Cuba and the Florida Keys, then stood north past Bermuda and crossed the Ocean Sea, running before the wind past the Azores to the bar of the Guadalquivir River at Sanlúcar de Barrameda. There the leather-encased box holding the painted book would have been handed over the side to a launch that would take it upriver to Seville; and then, once again by mule back, it would catch up with the peripatetic court somewhere in Spain and be delivered to the monarch himself.

Apart from the seasonal threat of heretofore unheard of — and previously unnamed — *huracanes* (a Taino word), as well as the ever-present dangers of uncharted reefs, scurvy, and disorderly crews, the Atlantic crossing exposed the vessels to French, Portuguese, and English corsairs. Small wonder that other Mexican artifacts mentioned in letters and inventories as packed for shipment never made it to their European destination.

One can easily imagine, in a Spanish bureaucracy famed for the volume of its paperwork, an exchange of receipts and shipping inventories among crown officials, the ship's captain, and the customs house in Seville — or even an inquisitor's stamp. The archives contain shipping lists even of ordinary books in the Atlantic trade. But from the day our "master of painters" cleaned up his brushes, handed the painted folios over to the supervising clergy, who in turn gave the book to the viceroy, who sent it on its way, there is no clear record of the Codex Mendoza. Not, that is, until the codex appeared, seemingly out of the blue, several years later in France. In fact, there is still doubt about the conventional story that the Codex Mendoza was taken off a captured Spanish vessel during the Atlantic crossing by a French pirate.

In 1553 the Frenchman André Thevet, later to be the *cosmographe du roi*, had something that sounds like the Codex Mendoza. Was this the same document seen by the Spaniard in the house of the Indian Gualpoyogualcal in 1547? Scholars agree that Richard Hakluyt did indeed acquire the Codex Mendoza from Thevet forty years later, in 1587; and from then on its trajectory is on firmer ground, ending, as we know, in the Bodleian Library. Even then, however, it lay there unknown to von Humboldt and other savants interested in ancient Mexican culture for nearly two centuries until Lord Kingsborough's obsessive search brought it into public view in the 1830s.

Thus the early history of both the Codex Mendoza and the Telleriano-Remensis is unknown. Beyond the assumption that the Telleriano-Remensis was produced in Mexico, little else can be inferred about its provenance. "Who first commissioned the manuscript, precisely where, when, why, and by whom it was made, the date and means by which it was conveyed to Europe, the country to which it was first taken, are questions that lack definitive answers."[6] The mystery surrounding these two very famous documents of New World history makes the obscure past of the Codex Cardona seem a bit less unusual.

Perhaps a paper trail will turn up evidence of the Codex Cardona's early colonial origins. At the moment we have only a casual remark by the Jesuit Francisco Calderón (included in Anthony Pagden's evaluation of the codex in chapter 9) that in 1630 he had presented to the Mexican viceroy two old post-Cortesian maps (one of the region of Lake Texcoco in the valley of Mexico) and a book that presented a historical account with figures and explanations in Spanish. Although this book was important enough to be presented to the viceroy and might have been the Cardona, Calderón's remark isn't evidence on which you'd want to bet the farm.

Questions linger about both the Codex Mendoza and the Telleriano-Remensis—and many other lesser codices. We cannot know how many other codices, maps, and documents—not to mention the millions of silver coins that by the late sixteenth century were pouring out of Mexican and

Peruvian mines—never made it across the Ocean Sea to Europe. Because the Cardona, like the Codex Mendoza, was commissioned at the highest levels of the royal bureaucracy, it was likely directed to the King's Council of the Indies in Seville. There is no record, however, of such a transaction, no indication of its presence in Spain or any place else in Europe or America until 1982.

I should mention one final codex, which was produced somewhat later than the Mendoza or Telleriano-Remensis and also followed a wandering migratory path. The *Historia general de las cosas de la Nueva España*, later known as the Florentine Codex, was completed in Mexico in 1577. It treats, among other things, the gods and goddesses worshiped by the Indians of Mexico, their feasts and rituals, their intellectual life, their moral and natural philosophy, and their commerce, artisans, and political life.

Almost unbelievably, its twelve books, contained in three volumes, are the work of one man, the remarkable Spanish Franciscan friar Bernardino de Sahagún. He not only compiled (with the help of native informants) what scholars have called, *avant la lettre*, an ethnographic work, and not only wrote the complete work in Nahuatl, but then translated his opus into Spanish. Alas, however, his Spanish monarch, Philip II, was not pleased. In a royal decree Philip ordered the Mexican viceroy to confiscate the work together with whatever copies there may have been and send them to the Council of the Indies in Seville for examination. The king added that "no one was to be permitted to describe the superstitions and customs of the ancient Indians"—for fear, presumably, that their descendants would find them attractive.[7]

The following year, however, in the autumn of 1578, the *Historia general*, apparently not confiscated—or if so, quickly released—arrived in Madrid. Just how the work got from there to the Laurentian Library in Florence (hence its present name, the Florentine Codex) ten years later is not certain. The most likely explanation is that Philip II sent one of his courtiers, don Luis de Velasco, to congratulate Cardinal Ferdinando de Medici, the new grand duke of Florence, on his ascension and also to try to arrange a political marriage between a daughter of the Medici clan and a worthy Spaniard. The new Medici duke was not only a collector of rare and exotic manuscripts but also the founder of the College for the Propagation of the Faith, which eventually took over most Catholic missionary activity around the globe. Consequently a modern scholar speculates that Sahagún's great work "would have been an obvious complement to the Duke's interests."

Moreover, the courtier Luis de Velasco was the son of the second viceroy of Mexico, and since he had lived there, in the viceregal palace, as a young man between 1560 and 1587, "he undoubtedly was acquainted with Sahagún." The strong circumstantial evidence that the *Historia general* was a gift carried by Velasco to the grand duke is supported by the fact that Sahagún's work soon turned up in the Laurentian Library in 1588, where it is today.[8]

CHAPTER THREE

Early Doubts

The absence of romance in my history will, I fear,
somewhat detract from its interest.

THUCYDIDES, *History of the Peloponnesian War*

 All of that—the first sighting of the Codex Cardona and my early fascination with the project—took place, as I've said, in 1985. A reasonable reader might ask why my initial enthusiasm so quickly dimmed and why I only picked up the threads of my research in 2004.

A few months after the events in the Crocker Lab, the Stanford negotiations failed and Thomas Schwarz packed up the codex and carried it off to an unknown fate. I tried to get in touch with the two principal Stanford professors I'd met that day at the Crocker Lab, but neither Jim Fox nor his colleagues were inclined to welcome my inquiries. They had been keen for Stanford to acquire the codex and perhaps were disappointed when the university didn't come through. Their Special Collections Department was troubled not only by doubts about the book's authenticity but also by the question of provenance—and the price, between six and seven million, was steep. The information given out by Schwarz, Professor Fox told me, was scant and would be of little use. He and his colleagues had "turned the page." My follow-up telephone call was not returned. At the same time, Schwarz had disappeared. I scoured several likely telephone directories and the rare books and manuscript catalogs in those pre-Google years, but with no success.

After 1986, the owner withdrew the Cardona from public view for fourteen years until May 1999 when it appeared at Christie's in New York—and then promptly disappeared—leaving no trace.

However, I couldn't get the mystery of the codex out of my mind. I continued rather desultory reading about early Mexico and became something of an *amateur* on codices. I talked a lot—too much—about the "mysterious Cardona," as I described it at dinner parties, and should have been mindful of Hemingway's warning how "talking out" a project diminishes the listener's interest. Besides, my headlong, if brief, plunge into the Cardona mystery meant that my other academic projects had suffered. I had research grants to obtain, a different book to write, students to teach.

My own professional life led to five years (from 2000 to 2004 with brief interruptions) as the director of the University of California's Education Abroad Study Center in Santiago, Chile; I also taught graduate courses in that city's Catholic University. Upon my return, inspired by a friend and colleague's enthusiasm and vivid speculation, I turned again to the story of the Cardona; following various tips and rumors and diverse strands of inquiry, I discovered that the codex had first appeared at Sotheby's London in 1982, and later, in 1985, at the Getty Museum in Los Angeles. I found and interviewed Mr. Schwarz, the owner's agent, and followed the trail of a mysterious affidavit to Seville and to Princeton University's Firestone Library to obtain fascinating information (with inconclusive results, however).

Then, on January 1, 2006, an inconspicuous but ultimately dramatic and completely unanticipated posting on the Internet—"un codice es mucho más . . ." ["a codex is much more . . ."]—led to striking, if fortuitous, discoveries. Thereafter, the pace of this story accelerates.

Soon after I returned to California in 2004, my friend and colleague David Sweet from Santa Cruz came up for the weekend. I'd first met David many years earlier in 1974, at a history conference in Monterey. He didn't attend the sessions that day but rather sat in a chair propped against the flowery pale green wall of a hotel corridor where large groups of students from the nearby campus gathered on the carpet, their eyes shining with fervent admiration, hanging on every word as David described the criminal nature of capitalism and the need for popular organization. He is tall and good-looking, with a head of curly hair, a terrific talker and full of ideas. David had so many irons in the fire that it was hard for him to select a single one for the scholarly anvil. But he had thought through a great many things, and though he is younger than I am, I quickly saw him as my mentor. David had no time for cynicism; he believed that frank and understanding talk dissolved personal problems and that verbal exploration of intellectual matter led to wisdom.

I went down to Santa Cruz a few times after that first meeting for conferences and graduate seminars and usually looked David up. One afternoon we took the first of what would be many long walks, this time among the pungent groves of eucalyptus in the hills above the campus. Dry leaves crackled underfoot, and an autumnal haze hung over Monterey Bay. David walked briskly, hands clasped behind his back, voluble, eloquent, knowledgeable, open. In the months and years to come, we visited each other's houses, met in San Francisco and Berkeley and Glen Alpine Canyon up near Tahoe for walks and talk, and came to share not only our public and scholarly concerns but also edged into our private lives as well. We mentioned the Codex Cardona's appearance or the Crocker Lab from time to time, but only in passing.

After breakfast on Saturday of the weekend of his visit, David's *compañera* went off to the farmers' market and the new health food store while he and I walked in the foothills west of the house. The rolling pastureland had turned wispy and pale yellow in the fierce sun. Along the fence line huge eucalyptus trees rustled faintly in the breeze. Cattle grazed among the scrub oak. Several Hereford heifers idly nibbled on the dried grass and some distance off a single indolent bull, his sexual appetite apparently slaked, ambled about aimlessly. We walked, stopped to make points, and went over, without much enthusiasm, recent reviews of books in our field, who was skewering whom, whose work was "penetrating" and even "seminal," and whose could be read with "interest" and "profit." We didn't use those terms, of course, except to lightly mock the clichés in book reviews; the last two, however, really did irritate David, who saw capitalism as the root of all evil.

Back at the house, David settled onto the sofa. Alex came in from the kitchen, fluffing up a spray of flowers from the garden. She seemed harried; she blew a wisp of hair out of her eyes with a quick upward puff out of the corner of her mouth and sat down. Her wheat-ripe hair was swept back into a thick braid. I was mentioning—again—the telephone conversation I'd had with Jim Fox all those years ago, how he'd told me that Schwarz and the codex had vanished and Stanford had lost interest. I admitted that I was still fascinated by what I had seen in the Crocker Lab. Alex rolled her eyes impatiently; she'd heard more than enough about this particular obsession. When she left the room, I went on about the Codex Cardona, how I couldn't get it out of my mind, how it really was a great project for someone. I recalled how I'd turned the pages, felt the crackle of the ancient *amate* folios, been knocked out by this extraordinary document, and so on.

I had told David about the Cardona when I first saw it, but now I dwelt on its paintings and remarkable maps. I said again that it was surely an extraordinarily valuable document, maybe even unique in its wealth of detail concerning the early encounter of the Aztecs with the Spaniards and a vital source in understanding the fatal conflict between Europeans and Indians after the invasion of America in the sixteenth century.

David asked questions and got caught up in the excitement as my own renewed enthusiasm escalated. He showed off a bit by displaying his knowledge even about the arcane subject of Mexican codices, which was not a specialty of either one of us.

"So it deals with the whole Valley of Mexico, then, or just Tenochtitlán, or what?" he asked.

"I didn't see the whole thing," I said, "just the pages that Schwarz turned for us, and I didn't have that much time with them. And of course the text is in the sixteenth-century hand, so I had to rely on the Stanford professors — one of them could read it like the newspapers. There were sections that deal with that big dam — what is it, the Albarrada? — I know you're interested in water history."

"Albarradón," David said. "Actually, it's a breakwater."

"Yes, OK, and lots of information about Tlatelolco and that Franciscan *colegio*, the Santa Cruz. There are charming illustrations of some of the friars."

I filled David in on a few more details of the Cardona's subjects and repeated the doubts that the Stanford professors had raised: Was it authentic? And more perplexing, if not authentic, who could possibly have carried out such an elaborate, informed fraud? The forger would have to have been a brilliant scholar. We mulled that over for a while, imagining various scenarios.

Suddenly David leaped to his feet, pointed a finger at the high-beamed ceiling, and cried out, "Robert Barlow! It was Robert Barlow!"

I knew I should have known who Robert Barlow is or was — more evidence for David that I was unprepared in my field.

"OK," I confessed, "who's Robert Barlow?"

David explained that Robert Hayward Barlow had been a brilliant young American poet and anthropologist, had studied at Harvard and attracted the attention of Alfred Kroeber, the venerated anthropologist at Berkeley, and obtained an early Guggenheim fellowship for research in Mexico in the 1940s. Barlow then became the much revered and precocious whiz kid in Mesoamerican studies in Mexico City. He'd learned Spanish, of course, and was also a respected student of Nahuatl, the lingua franca of central Mexico before the arrival of the Spaniards, whose use continued, among the native people, for a long time afterward. In fact, Barlow had taught Nahuatl at the National University of Mexico, to the Mexicans.

Moreover, Barlow's scholarly work, David pointed out, was precisely centered on the native societies to the east and south of Lake Texcoco. Barlow had written a fundamental work on Tlatelolco—the sister city of the Aztec capital of Tenochtitlán dealt with at length in the Codex Cardona—and was famed for several other articles and research papers all centered on the Valley of Mexico in the sixteenth century. He died—David wasn't sure exactly when—around 1950; suicide, he thought, and he remembered a certain scandal about Barlow's death. I don't know *how* David knew all this gossip; I guess because he'd gone off to Mexico just out of Oberlin College and hung out with lots of young Mexican writers and political people in the sixties. And, he takes everything in; he's an even better listener than talker.

"Look," David said, "if *anyone* could have forged the Cardona, Barlow could have."

Besides, he explained, in the 1940s there were still lots of people, lots of Mexican Indians, Nahuatl-speaking scribes, who turned out realistic-looking colonial painted *amate* documents for tourists, not to mention the professional forgers who had a long history of selling fake copies of codices to libraries around the world. So a scholar such as Barlow, an expert on all kinds of ethnohistorical detail, might have laid out the elaborate plan of the Cardona, worked hand in hand with native artists to make the pictographs, and found one of the scholars who had long worked in the archives to do the annotations—or he could have done it himself.

We went to my study, clicked up Melvyl, the university's online catalog, and searched the library holdings for Robert Hayward Barlow. David was right. There were three books of youthful poetry, an early mystery based on a mythical land, and seventy-four other references having to do with research publications on sixteenth-century Mexica societies around the lake and specifically with the city of Tlatelolco. If you imagined the essential bibliography for a scholarly forgery of the Codex Cardona, this was it. Barlow had been born in 1918 and died in 1951 at thirty-three.

"But this is really far-fetched," I complained. "Why would such a distinguished young scholar risk his career? His reputation? And if you're going to fake something, why not a Vinland map, a single folded sheet of parchment, rather than 427 laborious pages of text and illustration? It doesn't make sense."

Yet the possibility of a Barlow—or a Barlow-type—forgery lingered in my mind. The Cardona had been offered for big bucks, and the timing was right; that is, if it had really been created after 1945, as a possibly flawed radiocarbon date in the Cardona file suggested. It's true that forgers have done all sorts of improbable things, and Stanford, in fact, had been suspicious of forgery.

My fascination with the Cardona had been on the back burner; indeed, the gas had been turned off. But now, listening to David's questions and speculation, the codex swam back into my ken. I doubted, however, that this high fantasy about Barlow would lead to any concrete evidence. I hadn't really stopped thinking about a way to write some kind of story about the Codex Cardona, but I was sure that I'd have to anchor the story in serious research. It was also true that David's inflamed imaginings were not only entertaining but also opened up some new ways to think about the story.

CHAPTER FOUR

Sotheby's of London

The Cardona's maps struck Professor Pagden as particularly
impressive; they were "of the utmost importance . . .
the greatest rarity."

 As the year went on, David's visits became more frequent, and the Cardona became a common topic between us. He was focusing his considerable intellectual energy, getting fired up about the story behind the codex. He encouraged me to go to Mexico immediately, to take a sabbatical leave if I had to, and to find out all I could about rare book and antiquities dealers, but above all to spend several months in the National Archive tracking down documents that might bear on the Cardona. "You need to know, for example, if there really was an Alonzo Cardona y Villaviciosa in sixteenth-century Mexico, and those records are in the archive." More research was always David's solution to any query. His exuberant ideas are like earthworms; cut them in half and both ends grow, and they in turn divide again, with the result that his study is overstuffed with yellowing stacks of notes and photocopies, rows of books practically running down to the sea, but little of this finds its way into print.

"You have to be serious," he said more than once, "you have to be *consecuente*. Neither one of us knows enough about codices, but *you* have *lots* of work to do. You think the Barlow business is far-fetched, but there's no way you can ignore his collected papers. Apart from our speculation, he *did* specialize on the material covered in your codex.

"The papers," David added, "are in the University of the Americas in Puebla."

How did he know this? I wondered. Was he doing his own research?

David's speculations about the Cardona *were* interesting, but also unsettling, not only for wildly imputing base motives to such a revered person as Robert Barlow, but also because David's enthusiasms for endless research made any thought of actually carrying out the project quite overwhelming. It's true that I was a little anxious not knowing if I should—or, more to the point, if I were able—to take on the Cardona. I had accumulated many pages of notes, jotted-down musings and vague ideas, but no proper plan. The idea of archival research made my arms droop with fatigue—and talk about blind groping: the codex could be *anywhere*. I'd no doubt have to make a couple of trips to Mexico, maybe Spain, even London, particularly if behind Schwarz's vague statements it was true that the codex had been acquired by the present owner in Britain.

But where to start? I had by now learned quite a lot about Mexican codices, but the story I was really interested in was a *quest*, the search for the document itself. For me the adventure had begun that August afternoon in 1985 when I saw the codex spread out on a steel table in the Crocker Laboratory. I'd heard comments that day about the document's value, along with mysterious remarks about provenance by an unlikely book dealer. But that wasn't much. The few notes I was able to jot down that night after Schwarz's presentation to the Stanford professors wouldn't get me far.

Still, I'd been conscious that day of having come across something infinitely precious when I laid hands on the Codex Cardona, the kind of artifact one usually sees only under thick glass display cases in guarded museums. Moreover, if real, the Cardona was an invaluable account of the most dramatic encounter between Europeans and Native Americans in the Western Hemisphere, and I might be the one to bring it into public view. I couldn't help wondering, though: had I really felt with my own hands the coarse *amate* folios painted hundreds of years ago by long-forgotten Aztec craftsmen—or was it an exquisite forgery?

With my courses organized and the new term under way, I decided to begin my second push on the Cardona project by going back to the beginning, and perhaps, as the poet says, to know the place for the first time. Stanford was the last place, after all, that the codex had been seen, and there would surely be some files on the negotiations, even if Professor Fox had not been forthcoming. I'd also noticed that Gordon Brotherston, England's well-known expert on Mexican codices, had just come to Stanford, visiting from the University of Essex.

Fox was not eager to talk with me at first, but I insisted, and after two or three rather abrupt phone calls, we agreed on September 20, 2005, as a date for lunch. He agreed to ask Brotherston to join us and said he might even be able to dig up some old files on the Cardona. He remembered that a colleague had surreptitiously managed to photograph some of the folios with a hand-held camera and perhaps he could find and copy the photos. Fox had no idea where either Schwarz or the codex might be.

"Presumably, back to the owner, whoever that is," he told me. "It's not come up on my screen since that time you're talking about. It just disappeared."

I drove down the Bayshore Freeway, got off on Embarcadero Road in Palo Alto, scouted about for a parking place, and made my way to the steps up from a sunken campus circle road where we'd agreed to meet. Walking together to Fox's office, he unexpectedly became quite jolly, talking about his graduate studies in Chicago, about his seven children, about being a Mormon. He remarked in good humor that he was "the only Republican" in the Department of Anthropological Sciences, "maybe even in the entire faculty."

In his office, Fox was as pleasant as he looked, his spiky telephone manner very much softened. We went over that day in the Crocker Lab and agreed that Schwarz seemed an unlikely rare book dealer (I didn't mention the torn folio corner) and that several Stanford faculty members had been really keen on the Cardona. He said that he and three others "had formed ourselves into a small committee, thinking that if it turned out to be authentic, we would recommend that Stanford buy it."

"We had some background material to go on," Fox said, "a couple of reports from two unidentified earlier attempts—which we didn't know about—to sell the codex. Later, some disquieting information came in that the Cardona had failed two radiocarbon tests, one made in Cambridge and another in Florida, as I remember."

"What does 'failed' mean?" I asked.

"Well, again, as I recall, it meant that in one test the dates were 2045 BP [before present], plus or minus 50 years, which was clearly wrong; in the other, the Cardona was classified as 'modern'—that is, post-1945."

Obviously something must be terribly wrong about those dates, he continued. "It was a Florida lab—the Beta Analytic Lab in Coral Gables. We had several exchanges with the lab people, and they came back saying that their analysis might have picked up the readings from the protective varnish on the folios, which in turn might have been contaminated by fallout as a result of atomic weapons testing or from the Hiroshima and Nagasaki bombs themselves. It seems that sensitive radiocarbon dating tests can detect the presence of fallout in the most remote areas of the planet."

"Anyway," Fox continued, "although the radiocarbon tests were inconclusive, they still raised doubts. Tom Schwarz even mentioned that after the tests came in, the owner, or his agent, indicated some willingness to negotiate the price. I should say *more* doubts because the overall documentation was shaky. We can ask Gordon about his own experience at Sotheby's in London."

"I hadn't known it was at Sotheby's," I said.

"Neither did we," Fox said, "until Gordon told us."

"What about the other tests, the ones on ink and paper, that the Crocker Lab ran?"

"They weren't that useful," Fox said. "There was nothing dramatic." Cahill and Schwab's lab assistant had signed the final report showing that the inks were composed mainly of vegetable material. Unfortunately, the PIXE procedure only picks up mineral content. The paper had traces of calcium, iron, zinc, and strontium consistent with the mineral content found in a fifteenth-century Mexican codex fragment, examined for comparative purposes, held at the Bancroft Library in Berkeley. As for the pigments used in the Cardona, the Crocker Lab people thought they had the kind of content one would find in a sixteenth-century document. Nothing stood out as being of recent manufacture; but that didn't prove that it was sixteenth century. The Stanford people did learn that the paper was heavily impregnated with salt, but von Hagen's work on ancient Mexican papermaking shows that salt water from Lake Texcoco was commonly used in pre-Columbian papermaking—as it is today.

"Really," Fox said, "despite all these quibbles, we all thought there was a good chance that the codex was authentic; that is, a mid-sixteenth-century document as advertised, and we'd have *loved* to have had it here, even though my colleagues knew that the study of it would occupy several careers. But the doubts about the tests and the fact that Schwarz wouldn't name the owner spooked our Special Collections people and the provost. And the price was a bit high even for Stanford. We understood that it had been offered previously, but at that time we didn't know where, for $8 million. But Schwarz did suggest that the owner might be prepared to negotiate, since he was becoming impatient."

Fox looked at his watch. "Look," he said, "I still have a file on all this and could probably dig it up and share some of it with you now that we've definitely turned the codex down. But we should go now—Gordon will be over at the Faculty Club."

Gordon Brotherston was patiently waiting. A slight, balding Englishman with a mid-Atlantic accent, he had a healthy appetite. The Stanford Faculty Club buffet stretched out in parallel rows, each one many yards long, offering delicacies never seen in most of the University of California's campuses, not even in Berkeley. Gordon at first seemed more interested in the food than in my questions. He came back from the buffet with a full plate and sat down next to Fox.

"Yes," he said, "I was in on the Sotheby's presentation and so was Anthony Pagden. You'd be very interested in his opinion if you can find it; usually auction houses and museums are guarded about such things."

He turned away from me and engaged Fox in the inevitable academic gossip about local promotions, hirings, and firings, this time concerning a woman friend who was being mistreated by her department. After a few minutes, Brotherston pushed back his chair and headed back to the dessert line. I wondered if I would get anything useful out of him. I had to remember, too, that it had been twenty years since he'd seen the codex.

Despite his initially distracted and offhand manner, I knew that Brotherston was a renowned specialist in Aztec and early colonial painted books. And he had been one of the first people to see and offer an evaluation of the Cardona—the first time, as far as Fox and I were aware, that the book had come into public view. He had been in at the beginning of the Cardona's saga, and I was dying to get his opinion of the codex itself.

Brotherston told us that the Codex Cardona had simply emerged out of the London fog in 1982 when someone—he was never told who, although he'd heard rumors of a carpet and tapestry salesman—walked into Sotheby's, plunked the book down on a desk, and asked that it be placed on consignment for auction at eight million dollars. Until that time, not a single folio of the codex had been known to exist, no part of it had ever been published or recorded, nor today does the academic literature make a single reference to it. Moreover, as we sat in the Stanford Faculty Club that day, no one had any idea where the Cardona was or who claimed present ownership. Brotherston had heard vague and contradictory murmurs at Sotheby's about "a Hispanic gentleman resident in London," and another time that an Englishman had acquired it from a "Spanish family" also "resident in London." This, of course, more or less matched Schwarz's tale in the Crocker Lab.

For Brotherston, the kind of paper on which the Cardona was painted raised serious questions about the book's authenticity. As we have seen, the paper used in the Cardona was *amatl*—or, in Spanish, *amate*—made from the bark of an American variety of fig tree that had been used by native Mexican codex makers for many years, reaching back long before the sixteenth-century European arrival. *Amate* was the most common kind of paper found in pre-Columbian codices, but European paper quickly replaced it in the years following the Spanish conquest, particularly for the most important official documents. As I'd already learned, both the Codex Telleriano-Remensis and the Mendoza, mid-sixteenth-century contemporaries of the Codex Cardona, were painted on European paper and bear the watermark of a type of paper commonly imported to Spain from Genoa in the sixteenth century.

But rather than the European paper that Captain Cardona's *tlahcuilos* might have been expected to use—particularly for an official work ordered by the viceroy himself—the Indian artists of the Codex Cardona drew and painted on *amate*. In the 1550s, European paper would have been available. Why, then, Brotherston wondered, was Codex Cardona on *amate*? Perhaps because it was impossible for a modern forger to find enough sixteenth-century European folios, just as it was difficult for the forger of the Vinland map to find fifteenth-century parchment?

Stanford student waiters brought coffee to the table. Brotherston warmed to the paper problem, pointing out that any forger would have been inclined to use *amate* to avoid the problem of European paper, which normally carries a watermark and can be dated. Then too, he pointed out, there are repeated apologies by the scribe (or scribes) in the Cardona text itself for having to use *amate* instead of the more expensive and scarcer European paper, almost as if a forger would have expected a future buyer at Sotheby's or Stanford to raise those questions.

"I thought the scribes doth protest too much," Brotherston said.

"Look," he continued, "I was fascinated by the Cardona and could hardly believe my eyes when I saw it at Sotheby's; but the paper question, the fact that there was no previous record of the document—I mean, something like this just doesn't disappear for four or five hundred years—made me suspicious. I felt that the 1554 date must in any circumstances be bogus; as for the paper, I had been reliably informed that there could not be much doubt but that it is of quite recent origin." Brotherston did not recall the name of his reliable informant, nor exactly why the year 1554 had sent up a red flag.

Because the Cardona had first been offered to Sotheby's in London, I asked Fox if he had the impression that Schwarz had brought the Codex to Stanford from England. Fox said he didn't know. The Stanford Special Collections people knew only that Schwarz had made an appointment, knocked on their door, and presented the piece. Just as at the Crocker Lab, Schwarz had mentioned an owner, "resident in England."

We finished our coffee. Fox had a class to teach, so I left him at his office door, made my way up the Bayshore, and drove in thick traffic across the Bay Bridge and home. Back in my office, I wrote to thank Fox for his help and reminded him that he'd mentioned some files that he might be able to let me see.

There was no immediate response. I figured Fox must have been pretty busy with his seven children. After a couple of weeks, I left two messages on his phone. No response to those either, but a few days later I received in the mail a copy of the evaluation that Anthony Pagden, a distinguished specialist in early colonial history at Cambridge, had written for Sotheby's. Brotherston had found it in his files after our luncheon date. Schwarz had not included this document in the packet he'd brought to the Crocker Lab, which was strange, since Pagden had an enormously positive opinion of the Cardona. Perhaps the owner didn't want Schwarz to know that the codex had previously been offered to Sotheby's?

Pagden's opinion, comprising eight double-spaced typed pages, was enthusiastic, calling the Codex Cardona a document "of incalculable importance," an "extremely important and hitherto unknown Mexican manuscript . . . extensively illustrated throughout with maps, plans, portraits and depictions of topographical and historical scenes . . . written, on the order of don Antonio de Mendoza, first Viceroy of New Spain, and the Inspector General don Alonzo de Cardona de Villaviciosa . . . finished by his son don Juan de Cardona . . . and completed in 1554." "It is, in effect," Pagden wrote, "a Mexican Doomsday Book." The Cardona's maps struck Professor

Pagden as particularly impressive; they were "of the utmost importance . . . the greatest rarity."

Before the Cardona there are only three important known maps of early Mexico-Tenochtitlán (the Mexico City of today). The first is the Nuremberg map, so called because it was first published in Nuremberg in 1524 in the preface to a Latin edition of the *Segunda carta de relación* that Hernán Cortés sent to Charles V from "Temixtitlan-Mesyco" in 1520. Scholars have written a lot about this map, but to this day we don't know whether the map was redrawn from a native image that found its way from Mexico to Europe or whether it derives from a European "imaginative visual reinterpretation" of Cortés's own description as contained in his *Segunda carta.*[1]

The second early map is a plainly named and rudimentary drawing of a section of Mexico-Tenochtitlán, the *plano en papel de maguey,* or "map on maguey paper," now held in the National Museum of Anthropology and History in Mexico City. The third, dated 1550 and sometimes known (erroneously) as the Santa Cruz map, is at the University of Uppsala, Sweden. Alonzo de Santa Cruz was a famed mapmaker, Charles V's geography teacher, and royal cosmographer to Charles's son, Philip II.

In his evaluation for Sotheby's, Pagden wrote that the Cardona map was made in Mexico and, like the text of the codex itself, painted on *amate.* Pagden called the map "the greatest existing historical document recording the early colonial history of Mexico." The Uppsala map, in contrast, was made in Spain on parchment, apparently of deerskin. It measures 114 by 78 centimeters; the Cardona map of Mexico-Tenochtitlán, when its four elephant (oversize) folios are unfolded and spread out, extends to 114 by 90 centimeters—about the same size. The Cardona map, Pagden wrote, is a worthy complement, and in many ways superior, to the Uppsala map in its depiction of streets, canals, causeways, and architectural details.

More importantly, the Cardona map was drawn from firsthand observation in Mexico, whereas an entire ocean stretched between Philip II's royal cosmographer in Madrid and the city imagined from written accounts to be Mexico-Tenochtitlán. Pagden remarked that the Mexico City map—indeed, the entire corpus of maps in the Cardona—is a discovery "quite without parallel."

In his evaluation, Pagden also laid out his own list of subjects taken up by the scribes and painters of the Cardona: "Indians are shown at work, sowing, reaping, cooking, fishing, carving out a boat, tilling soil, grinding corn, rowing a boat, digging irrigation systems, building a church, paying taxes and tribute, cutting the maguey plant to make fabric along with other tasks together with their native tools and implements, baskets, storage bins, clothing, and head-dresses."

Also shown in the Codex Cardona were the effects of one of many plagues, probably the smallpox epidemic of 1545, and the cremation of corpses, along with depictions of the crimes and vices, such as theft and fornication, of the native people. Maybe this, I thought, is what Schwab, back at the Crocker Lab, had considered "pornographic." Vivid illustrations showed the dramatic encounter between Cortés and Moctezuma; others displayed Cortés and his ill-fated Spanish wife. (There were always rumors that he had strangled her or had her poisoned.) The Cardona, as we have seen, has one illustration of the conqueror himself carrying a corner of her casket with some accompanying text that I was unable to decipher that day at the Crocker Lab.

Pagden gave other examples of the codex's content. A friar, identified as "Fray Tomás," is shown burning heretical Indian books and manuscripts, "libros e papeles . . . que tractan de Herexias e cosas del demonyo" (books and papers that deal with heresies and the devil's things); we also see the whipping of a "disobedient" Indian and the Spanish supervision of Aztecs building a church. We see Viceroy Mendoza ordering the layout of a new town, and his successor, Viceroy Luís de Velasco, supervising Indian workers in the construction of the monumental Albarradón, the four-mile-long flood barrier anchored in Lake Texcoco southeast of the Aztec capital.

"These remarkable sketches," Pagden wrote, "provide vivid detail on daily life and heretofore-unknown information about a great, Crown-supervised hydraulic project in early Mexico." He summed up his evaluation as follows:

> Without doubt the Codex Cardona is the most important source in the early colonial history of Mexico to have come to light in the present [twentieth] century. With its account of the geography of the valley of Mexico and of contemporary Indian life, its detailed maps and street plans and its pictorial representations of topographical and historical subjects, this manuscript is a unique and incomparable source of information. Its implications for scholarship will undoubtedly be felt by students in History, Anthropology, Cartography and other fields of research for many years to come. A comparison with other Mexican codices of the sixteenth century made with the same material (for instance the Selden

Roll in the Bodleian Library at Oxford) leaves no doubt as to the authenticity of the Codex Cardona.

Moreover, Pagden added, "several mid-sixteenth-century buildings and the remains of canals and stone bridges shown in the Cardona have only recently, since the 1980s, come to light as a result of excavations for subway or telephone lines in the heart of the ancient city, and could not have been known by anyone except a very recent forger."

Despite this endorsement by such a distinguished scholar, Sotheby's had chosen not to accept the Cardona on consignment, perhaps because of Brotherston's hesitation regarding the paper and, no doubt, because of the questions that arose over provenance and authenticity.

Apart from information regarding the content of the codex, my knowledge of the actual circumstances of the Cardona's appearance at Sotheby's was scant. Neither Brotherston nor Pagden was told who represented the Cardona to Sotheby's; nor were they ever told where the codex had come from or the name of the owner. A few days after I read his report, I phoned Pagden. His memory was somewhat faint, but he did remember that he'd worked with a woman named Priscilla Thomas at Sotheby's. I found that she had gone to live in Australia, but beyond that there was no further public record. My own request to Sotheby's for information was politely but firmly rejected. Auction houses, museums, and collectors are understandably reluctant to give out confidential information, particularly at long distance, and at the time I wasn't prepared to invest in air travel to London to pursue the matter on the ground.

I later learned from another specialist, the late professor H. B. Nicholson, known by his colleagues at UCLA as "Mr. Codices," that the Cardona had been displayed in a confidential, private showing organized by Sotheby's at the International Congress of Americanists in Manchester. Nicholson told me he was "amazed" by the Cardona, completely "fascinated"; but like Brotherston, he was put on guard because of the paper. Professor Nicholson died in 2007.

After displaying the Cardona for a few hours in a closed room at the Manchester conference in August 1982 and then failing to place the codex with Sotheby's, the owner—or owners—apparently withdrew the codex until it was offered to the Getty's Special Collections Department three years later, in 1985. I didn't have any knowledge of this, and Stanford had only heard rumors. During Schwarz's time at Stanford, including the event at the Crocker Lab, he had not offered any information about prior offerings or negotiations, and as far as the Stanford people knew, there was no record of other attempts to sell the Cardona either in Europe or in the United States.

During this time, unknown to Sotheby's and Gordon Brotherston—I found out much later—the Cardona's owner apparently brought the codex to the attention of one of Mexico's most wealthy businessmen, Emilio Azcárraga Milmo, who had put together the Televisa empire. Azcárraga's advisors, however, cautioned against purchase on the grounds of a "chemical examination of the paper" that suggested a twentieth-century origin of the *amate*. The examiners suspected that the codex might actually have been worked up by "an erudite person [*un erudito*] familiar with sources hidden away in libraries and archives." Consequently the sale fell through, not only because of these doubts but also because the "intransigent" owner wanted several million more than Azcárraga was prepared to pay.[2]

Usually, in the small, clannish world of the rare book and manuscript trade, word travels fast about a hot new item; but the Cardona, like Yeats's long-tailed fly upon the stream, seems to have moved upon silence. No doubt its appearance left a stir among a handful of specialists in London, but the news hadn't made it from Sotheby's across the Atlantic. More surprising, the Cardona had apparently not stirred any interest in the antiquities and book trade in Mexico itself. But that's understandable, since the attempted sale of such an item of national patrimony, if made public, might provoke official interest.

As for the many scholars who have devoted their intellectual lives to the study of early codices, not even the most knowledgeable Mexican specialists had heard of the Cardona, even after it had surfaced in London. H. B. Nicholson later told me that three or four other specialists had been in the room with him that day in the Manchester hotel, but no one, it seems, was permitted to photocopy a single page of the Cardona. There may be photocopies of certain pages of the codex—it's hard to believe that no one other than Fox's Stanford colleague yielded to that temptation—but none so far had come to light. Three years after the unsuccessful attempt to place the codex with Sotheby's, the Cardona was offered to the Getty's Special Collections Department in Los Angeles.

CHAPTER FIVE

The Getty

I recall my hands shaking with excitement. It was easy to imagine
the ancient Aztec hands that made this paper, turned these pages,
the painters and scribes who had laboriously compiled this record.
Where in the world, I wondered, had it been all these years?

STEPHEN COLSTON, July 20, 1985

 It became more and more apparent that the Codex Cardona
had a more mysterious and troubled past than I'd imagined. I called colleagues at UCLA, Texas, and Yale to inquire
about who might have been consulted for an opinion on the
Cardona. As I sat in the reading room of Berkeley's Bancroft Library, leafing through a collection of recent dissertations on Mesoamerican ethnohistory, a name fairly leaped off the page at me: a dissertation dedicated
"to the memory of Robert Barlow," written by Stephen Colston at UCLA in
1973. Barlow, of course, was the tragic scholar who had figured in my and
David's fanciful speculation about who could possibly have undertaken the
elaborate forgery of a sixteenth-century codex. A graduate student's dedication to a revered professor is not unusual, and Colston could hardly have
known a man who died in 1951; still, having speculated about Barlow, and
now to see his name in the dedication, suddenly made him seem real, not
an imaginary presence. In any case, Colston might be able to provide some
information about Barlow.

But then I saw that Colston's dissertation had little to do with ethnohistory—or codices—but rather dealt with the Dominican friar Diego
Duran. Duran was one of the more important chroniclers who lived in
sixteenth-century Mexico, but not a subject close to the Codex Cardona—
or, for that matter, close to Barlow. Nevertheless the coincidence, or rather
the imagined coincidence (I was grasping for straws at this point) made it

seem worthwhile to get in touch with Professor Colston. He was close at hand, at San Diego State University. The next day, 6 September 2005, I rang him. I had to clear my head about any imagined connection between Barlow and the Cardona so that he wouldn't think I was mad. I knew he wouldn't know anything about the Codex Cardona, but maybe he'd have something to say about Barlow, the man.

Colston was friendly, not impatient, on the phone. We talked a bit about our common interests and people we knew in the field. I tried to mention the dedication of his dissertation to Barlow as casually as I could, unsure of what it might elicit. Did I think he'd perhaps say, "Oh, yes, I dedicated my doctoral dissertation to the well-known forger, Robert Barlow"? What he *did* say was this:

"Yes, Robert Barlow was something of a hero of mine when I was starting out in Mesoamerican ethnohistory at UCLA, so, well, you already know—I dedicated my dissertation to him. He died before I was born, but I loved his work. In fact—I almost forgot—I have his picture on my office wall. He was an *exceptional* scholar, a gringo beloved by Mexicans and Europeans in a field where there's a great lot of rivalry and jealousy."

I brought up the rumors surrounding Barlow's suicide, but Colston didn't pick up on that. "Since you're interested in Barlow, though," he said, "I have a little anecdote about him. Several years ago I researched the movie *Captain from Castile*—I think it came out in the late forties—in the archives of the Academy of Motion Picture Arts and Sciences, and discovered that Barlow was a consultant for the film. He apparently wrote some of the Nahuatl dialogue for it. Maybe you know that Tyrone Power starred in the film and bought a big abandoned hacienda in Mexico while he was there filming."

Turning the talk to Colston's own work, I told him that I'd come across an interesting document more or less in his field, and asked if he'd ever heard of the Codex Cardona.

There was a long silence.

"Why do you ask?"

I explained about the Crocker Lab, the Stanford business, the doubts, and my own growing interest.

"Well, yes," he said. "In fact, I *did* have something to do with that a year ago when the Getty was interested in getting it for their collection. But I'm surprised you'd think of me in that connection. It's a long, sort of murky story. I'd have to dig in my files, since it's been a few years now and I don't know how much you want to know."

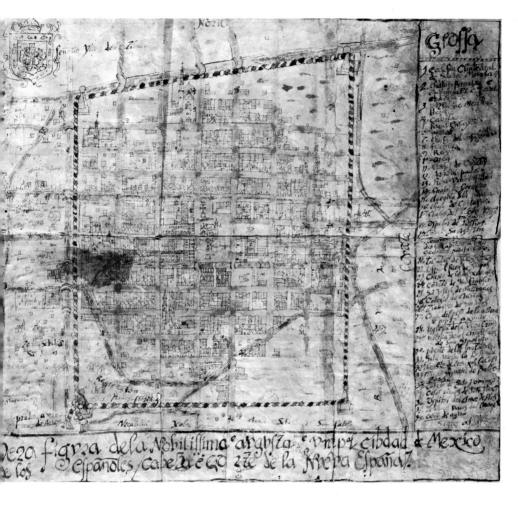

1   "True map of the very noble and imperial City of Mexico." Heretofore unknown
publicly, this is perhaps the first map ever made of Mexico City from on-site
observation. Painted on *amate*, the map measures 90 by 114 cm when unfolded.
The date is uncertain, perhaps ca. 1555–60. The so-called Dresden and
Uppsala maps, based on written accounts, are earlier.

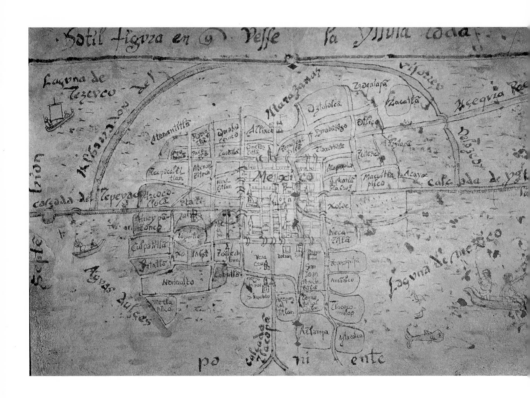

2   A heretofore unknown map of the Indian districts surrounding Mexico City, ca. 1550–55. The map is aligned with the east up. On the right is the causeway leading from Iztapalapa, entry point of the Spanish invaders in 1519; to the left is the causeway to Tepeyac, the future shrine of the Virgin of Guadalupe.

3   María Axixina (also known as Achichina). A drawing of a previously unknown
woman from Mexicaltzingo, who took part in an anti-Spanish conspiracy. Axixina
was subsequently hanged along with her co-conspirators, and her house was burned.
The Codex Cardona illustrates her tragedy in several pages.

4 (top at left) Antonio de Mendoza, first viceroy of
   Mexico (1535–49), shown directing the foundation
   of European-style Indian villages. Notice building
   techniques and early church construction.

5 (bottom at left) "True and accurate plot of the town
   of Mexicaltzingo." Mexicaltzingo was an important
   Culhua lordship (*señoría*) some eight miles south
   of Tenochtitlán. Note the heavy canal traffic of both
   Spanish sail and native canoes.

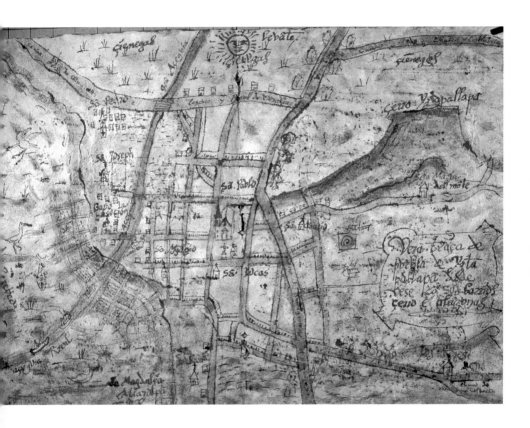

6   "True plot of the pueblo of Iztapalapa." The Cortés expedition passed though
     Iztapalapa, a town of some twelve thousand people, on November 8, 1519, along the
     "broad causeway" to Mexico-Tenochtitlán. The painting shows the Cerro, or Hill of
     the Star, where a fire ceremony solemnly took place to inaugurate a new "bundle"
     of fifty-two years of the Aztec calendar.

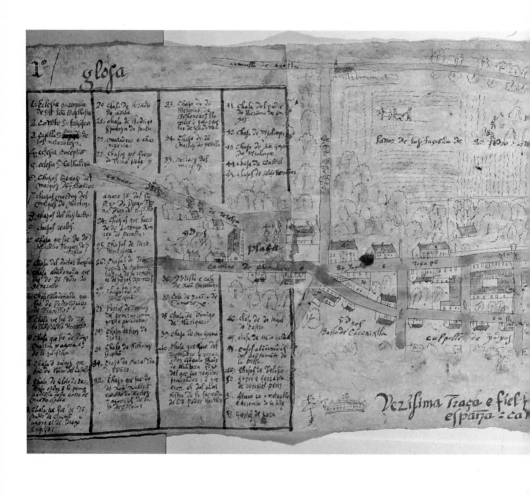

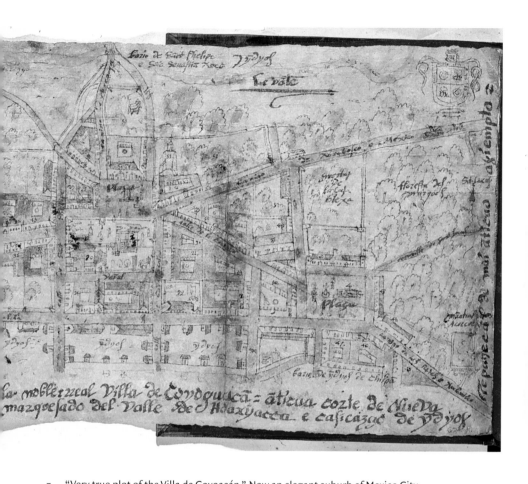

7   "Very true plot of the Villa de Coyoacán." Now an elegant suburb of Mexico City,
     in the first third of the sixteenth century, Coyoacán was a favorite residence
     for the first conquerors, such as Cortés, Bernal Díaz del Castillo, and
     Nuño de Guzmán. The map, on *amate*, indicates the location of these and
     other houses. The detail suggests a date of approximately 1555–56.

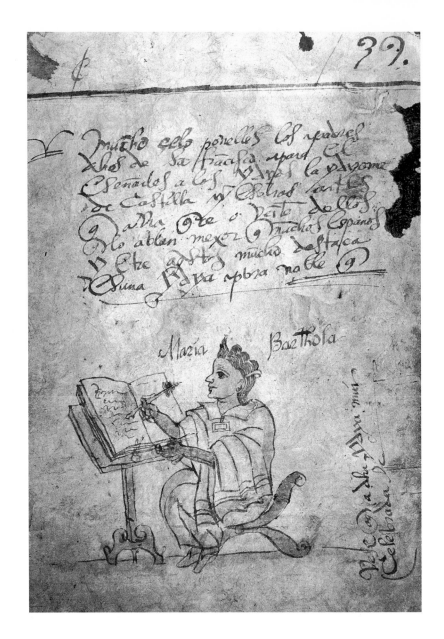

8   Doña María Bártola, a Christianized indigenous woman who wrote an account of
     Cortés's siege of Tenochtitlán. Her work is mentioned in an early-seventeenth-
     century work by Fernando de Alba Ixtlilxóchitl. The scribes of the Codex Cardona
     praise the work and depict doña María actively writing.

A pause. I could hear the swivel chair squeak in Colston's office. He must have been looking at the wall because he distractedly mentioned that he'd been given color prints of four of the charming painted birds in the Cardona from plates that the Getty had made during the negotiations over the codex. I imagined them hanging side by side with the photo of Barlow. Good God, maybe there *was* some sort of a curious connection between Barlow and the Cardona.

But why would I think that? All I had, I had to remember, was a connection between Colston and Barlow, nothing about Barlow and the Cardona. On the other hand, what had Barlow been doing with a movie company? Had he been desperate for money? Unlikely; by all accounts, he'd been a dedicated scholar living a spartan life.

It was clear that Colston was an important player in the story I was trying to put together, and I wanted to talk face to face. So I invented a trip—I didn't want him to think that I was *so* keen that I'd make a special trip—telling him that I would be in San Diego on university business later in the month and perhaps we could get together.

Colston arrived at the deli where we'd agreed to meet a bit before noon. He was a tall, substantial, earnest, and friendly man; and, I soon learned, nearly as fascinated about the Cardona as I was.

In December 1984, at a meeting sponsored by the Archives of American Art at the Huntington Library in Pasadena, Colston told me he had sat next to a distinguished gentleman who turned out to be Nicholas Olsberg, the head of Special Collections at the Getty Museum; Olsberg also held a position of authority in the Archives of the History of Art at the J. Paul Getty Center. Learning in the course of a casual conversation that Colston was a specialist in Mesoamerican material, Olsberg invited him to dinner at a posh restaurant called the Chronicle in Pasadena. "Not the sort of place I was accustomed to," Colston told me.

By the end of the evening, Olsberg mentioned that the Getty was interested in building its collection of early Americana and had sent buyers to Mexico and Peru. He briefly described the project at hand and proposed that Colston evaluate an "unusual and even suspect but most intriguing Mexican codex" that had come to the Getty's attention. The circumstances and procedure, Olsberg warned, "were not the customary ones."

"I remember thinking," Colston told me, "this has to be fate. I'm discussing the possibility of working on a Mexican codex that seems to be a chronicle, at a place called the Chronicle! I also recall what an elegant place it was . . . My eyes were filled with glimpses of beautiful women and my ears with talk of sixteenth-century Mexican codices."

Three weeks after the Huntington conference, Colston met with Olsberg in the reception room of Getty's Special Collections.

"I filled out the appropriate forms," he said, "and I remember handing over a ballpoint pen, key chain, and loose coins to a pleasant woman. I was taken to a modern reading room, all blond oak and high windows, temperature 71.5 degrees Fahrenheit, that looked across the manicured grounds." As Colston described it, I imagined an island of tranquillity in Los Angeles's roaring sea of traffic. After a few minutes, Olsberg appeared followed by two men in tie and vest who placed the Codex Cardona on a solid table along with a teak page turner the size of a lotus leaf, a magnifying glass, lined yellow paper, and several number four pencils.

After the two men left, Olsberg turned toward the codex, open arms extended. "So this is it," he told Colston.

"Olsberg said I should take my time," Colston told me. "If I thought I could help them out, they'd be pleased to have my opinion. Olsberg confessed that he knew little about the codex, nothing at all about the owner or where it had come from. But he was sure that the subject matter would be familiar to me. Olsberg said that as far as the Getty's research department has been able to determine, there was no public record or reference to a Codex Cardona, nor anything of similar content under a different name in libraries, in other special collections, or in the bibliographies they'd been able to consult."

Olsberg revealed that the codex had been placed on the market, or rather that an attempt had been made to place it on the market, at least once before. He mentioned that the bookseller had included one brief report and that the Getty had asked two other scholars in Colston's area of expertise for opinions.

"He emphasized that I would not be able to see the other reports: 'They're confidential; rules, you know.'" Olsberg mentioned one other thing. The owner, or rather the agent, had asked that the document be placed in a Wells Fargo safe-deposit box at a branch near the Getty—even though Olsberg pointed out that the Getty was as secure as any bank. But the owner insisted. "Finally," Colston said, "I was permitted to take the slides home and work with them in my house or office. There were exactly 692. Of course I'd have to return them, and Olsberg pointed out that it would be highly inappropriate to make copies."

Olsberg gave Colston papers to sign and asked that he give the Getty some idea of how much time he'd need. A target schedule might be five or six weeks. The Getty was particularly interested in the extent to which the codex provided new or unique material for the scholarly world; how it compared with similar pre-Hispanic or early colonial native codices; and if, in Colston's opinion, there was any evidence for authenticity or forgery. It was only fair to say, Olsberg told him, that some doubts had been raised. He added that Colston would be "adequately compensated."

After Olsberg left the reading room, Colston said, he turned the pages of the Cardona. Mostly he'd worked in his own research with copies of originals; but here, laid out in front of him, were not only some three hundred pages of spectacular paintings and maps, drawings of birds and feathers, daily life, clothing, and food, but an entire record of a people who had effectively disappeared over four centuries ago.

"I had no hesitation," Colston said, "in putting my own research aside and beginning my evaluation of the Codex Cardona for Mr. Olsberg."

The day after I returned to my office from San Diego, I rang Colston. He'd found a copy of his evaluation for the Getty and had mailed it to me. He thought I'd have it the next day.

In the evaluation, Colston, like Brotherston, was "perplexed" by the use of *amate* in place of European paper and also noticed that the folios appeared to have been sized and that in some cases the sizing (a kind of varnish) was thickly applied. Colston was skeptical about the use of *amate* for such an important work. "I know of no other colonial Mexican codex," he wrote in his evaluation, "the product of official Spanish patronage, that provides such a full expression of the codex tradition, that is composed on *amate* as is the Cardona. The other main contemporary ones are on European paper." He thought the Cardona an anomaly.

The "singular pictorial content" of the Cardona impressed Colston. He wrote that it offered insights into early Mexican colonial experience "in a way that is afforded by no other known source." He believed the codex to be the work of at least three different scribes and as many illustrators; if the Cardona were authentic, they were most likely native Aztecs, or if mestizos—the offspring of Spaniards and Indians—very young men, because they would have been born after the Spanish entry into Mexico in 1519. Most likely, he thought, they were somewhat Europeanized Indians, conversant with both native glyphs and Spanish book arts.

The Getty—just as Sotheby's had been earlier, and Stanford afterward—was naturally concerned with authenticity. The uncertain provenance and the question about paper were cause for worry. But in his conclusion, Colston wrote that "on the basis of the slides I examined, I found nothing which might challenge outright the authenticity of the Codex Cardona. Certainly, the use of native paper does not of itself suggest that the Codex is falsified but it does raise important questions about the manuscript's composition." At the same time, however, he made no claim that it *was* authentic, because his evaluation focused solely on the manuscript's style and content.

"Falsified Middle American pictorial manuscripts," Colston wrote, "have been acquired by individuals and institutions throughout the world." He referred to two scientific tests mentioned in the file Olsberg provided that were apparently going to be conducted at the Atomic Energy Research Establishment in Cambridge and by "chemical analysts affiliated with the Conservation Department at the British Museum," but pages were missing from the file itself. To the end of his report, Colston added a page-by-page inventory of the illustrations, noting that the codex was not complete; some thirty of the 427 pages were missing. This, I was surprised to notice, is something that neither Pagden's report for Sotheby's nor the scrutiny by Fox and his colleagues a year later at Stanford had reported.

Colston included with his evaluation a copy of a second opinion that Olsberg had passed on to him in the Getty packet. This was not so much a scholarly or professional evaluation as a three-page, undated, unsolicited letter, addressed "To Whom It May Concern." The letter testifies mysteriously "to the authenticity of a document that has been left to me for its examination." The letter, unsigned, is written by an architect, Guillermo Gutiérrez Esquivel, resident in Sierra Paracaima Street number 865, in the residential sector of Las Lomas de Chapultepec, Mexico City. The text is a clumsy translation from another language, presumably Spanish. Gutiérrez Esquivel describes himself as a central figure in the vast reconstruction of the Centro Histórico of Mexico City and the director of the restoration of the Franz Mayer, the jewel-like colonial museum a few blocks from the Palace of Fine Arts.

"Being intimately involved in the reconstruction of the old colonial capital," Gutiérrez Esquivel writes, "I am able to confirm the historical veracity of this document because many buildings, the remains of canals, even the early foundations of the metropolitan cathedral, that are shown in the Cardona's maps, did not come into public view until the 1980s." There is a personal note: "The fresco paintings in a house in Coyoacán that by coincidence is owned by my family and appear in the Codex . . . were unknown until now." The letter mentions in passing a well-known Mexican archaeologist, Francisco González Rul, who, it seems, saw the Cardona during the time he worked with Gutiérrez Esquivel on the restoration of the Centro Histórico project.

There is no explanation for the presence of this letter, or rather this translation of a letter, in the file. Colston didn't remember how it got there or whether Olsberg had requested it. It did cross his mind that the archaeologist González Rul or his team of excavators could have found the codex among the ruined sixteenth-century building they were restoring. It would not have been the first time such a thing had happened.

After Colston delivered his report to the Getty, Olsberg gave him a gift of a dozen color reproductions of the Cardona's folios that had been used by the committee charged with evaluating the codex for acquisition.

It took me a while to find Nicholas Olsberg. He had left the Getty a few years after the business with the Cardona. Colston had lost track of him, and his successor at the Getty was not helpful. After his work at the Getty, Olsberg had become the director of the Canadian Center for the Arts in Montreal. He showed up on the Internet in several conferences, but none of these provided either an e-mail address or a telephone number, let alone an ordinary mailing address. I checked telephone directories in several cities including Montreal and Santa Monica and finally, on a guess, imagined that he might have retired in Southern California; and indeed, he did turn up in the Santa Barbara phone book. I left a message; he was alive, and he rang me back.

"Yes, I certainly remember that document," Olsberg said, "but I'm retired now." He mentioned Stephen Colston's "fine" report. Olsberg actually was still interested—in fact, fascinated—by the Cardona and, after his initial reticence, was happy to talk to me about it. He said he'd first seen the codex at the house of the agent, Mr. Thomas Schwarz, in Santa Monica and believed that the illustrations, particularly the maps, were "spectacular."

Olsberg said that the reason the Getty didn't acquire the Cardona was not because of the cost—the agent was asking "only a few million," as he recalled—but because of the "quirky and murky" story of ownership and because the material did not fit that well with the Getty's collection policy at the time. He had the impression from Schwarz that the owner lived in London.

Olsberg thought that the issues of *amate* versus paper and the radiocarbon dates were not too important. As for real or false, Olsberg said that forgery was always a possibility, but he wondered "why anyone would go to such work to falsify over four hundred pages and such a large number of illustrations. The map, the large map of Mexico City, was worth a great lot by itself."

In parting, he asked me please to stay in touch with him. "You might also try Wim de Wit, who's still at the Getty and was also involved in the discussions. He might even have the large number of slides we looked at."

Wim de Wit was easy to find, since he was the current head of Special Collections and Visual Resources at the Getty. I explained my questions in an e-mail, asking particularly about the slides that Olsberg thought might still be in the Getty file.

"In general," Mr. de Wit replied, "we do not share these kinds of files."

I gently insisted in a second e-mail, saying that I had already seen the codex, had been given the name of the agent, seen evaluations, and so on. Perhaps, I suggested, he could look at the file and remove any items that were confidential or especially sensitive; there might still be something useful for the kind of inquiry I wanted to make. I added that I intended to be in Los Angeles next month and could pop by to look at things that might be useful to me but no longer of interest to the Getty.

On October 6, 2005, a couple of weeks later, Mr. de Wit responded: "Please excuse me for being out of touch so long. Work on exhibitions took up all my time during the last two months. I have gone through the files for the Codex Cardona and unfortunately had to decide that the materials in it are confidential. I hope you understand. I did find one note, however, that goes back to your original request. The box of slides was returned to the agent, Tom Schwarz. We didn't make those copies, they were provided to the Getty as part of the project. I suggest you ask Schwarz what happened to these slides."

Unfortunately, Thomas F. Schwarz seemed to have vanished from the earth. And like Schwarz, the Cardona had not been heard of after its appearances at Sotheby's, the Getty, and the Crocker Lab. It had become a phantom. Nothing appeared in a search of conferences where such an artifact might be discussed, no notice in research libraries. Why had the owner or his agent decided to withdraw the codex from the market? Or perhaps he hadn't. Maybe it had been offered to other auction houses or universities? Or—much more likely—it may have been sold to a private collector. But nothing, as far as I could determine, showed up in the rare book and manuscript trade.

Still, one had to think, not every collector, public or private, has six or eight million dollars lying around to buy a suspect Mexican codex; and if he or she did, there would probably be requests for expert opinions, and these can—although they hadn't in the Cardona's case so far—enter the academic and museum gossip circuit. That led to a disquieting thought. The Cardona's appearances at Sotheby's, the Getty, and Stanford did not attract wide attention; I'd only learned of the codex's appearance at the Crocker Lab through sheer accident because my colleague Richard Schwab happened to ask me along that day. This meant that the Cardona might already have been sold more than once or might adorn a private library or collection of any number of people. Or, a dark thought indeed, it might have been broken up and sold off in pieces, the maps and illustrations first, then the individual folios.

Another possibility, quite a long shot, is that the Cardona *really* is a falsification, not necessarily a modern one (although that's not out of the question) but a later colonial—say, eighteenth-century—creation made to look like an earlier work. This is something one sees in other colonial documents used to establish original land titles and family origins. If that's the case, maybe the word got around and the owner was stuck with an elaborate and worthless fraud, a simple curiosity. That, too, would make a good story, maybe even more intriguing and gripping than tracking down the real thing.

I had read, for example, *The City of Light*, published in a luxury edition by a respectable press (Little, Brown), and presented by David Selbourne, a well-known historian who, according to the dust jacket, "had taught the history of ideas at Ruskin College, Oxford, for two decades." The book was advertised as "one of the most important manuscripts ever discovered," a translation of one Jacob D'Ancona's "perilous voyage to the East," which presumably took place in 1260, four years before Marco Polo's epic travels in 1264–66. A year after *The City of Light* was published to wide acclaim, Jonathan Spence, a distinguished Chinese specialist at Yale, revealed the book, in spirited criticism, to be a fraud.

Why does anyone undertake the enormous effort of deception? Money, sometimes lots of money, provides one explanation, but not by any means the only one. Pride in scholarship and excessive devotion to an *idée fixe* drove an elderly Swiss Jesuit, an unlikely counterfeiter, to fake the Vinland map in the 1920s. The Piltdown man was a case of high jinks, an elaborate fraud aimed at embarrassing the scholarly world, not for money. In other cases, the delicious *frisson* that comes from putting something over on the would-be experts is a motivation.

Often the forgers are several steps ahead of the experts. Sir Francis Drake's famous memorial inscribed on a "plate of brass" and nailed to a post on a California beach in 1579 was proudly displayed by the University of California for fifty years and solemnly celebrated by dignitaries, including Queen Elizabeth II, on the four hundredth anniversary of Drake's circumnavigation. But it turned out that Drake's plate of brass had been fabricated from American Brass and Foundry's no. 8 bronze plate by a merry band of grownup San Francisco pranksters in the 1920s. They became so entangled in the caper—which attracted more national and international attention than they'd anticipated—that they were reluctant to come forward to confess. In 1980, a metals laboratory indelicately exposed the hoax during the same week the queen was celebrating Sir Francis's return to Plymouth.

The brilliant forgery of the Vinland map, drawn on authentic fifteenth-century parchment, in which even the wormholes were faked and cleverly lined up with those in the surrounding parchment of the *Tartar Relation* (of which the map was said to be a part), fooled the British Museum's experts, who spent seven years certifying, alas in error, the map's authenticity. The original book dealer in this case claimed that he had bought the map from a Spanish aristocrat who preferred to remain anonymous for fear of being taxed. Yale University acquired the map through the generosity of Paul Mellon, the Pittsburgh millionaire, with only the most flimsy evidence of provenance. Hence the emphasis on high-tech evaluation—too late, it turned out, in the Vinland case, to prevent the fraud.

Closer to home, closer to the world of Mexican codices, are the Techialoyans. Indian communities presented these documents, written in Nahuatl on *amate* paper in eighteenth-century late colonial courts as evidence of ancient ownership of village lands. The Techialoyans were accepted by litigants (and modern scholars) as legitimate sixteenth-century documents, and it was not until the mid-twentieth century that they were found to be exquisite forgeries, mass-produced to demonstrate the original power and influence of native settlements as heirs to indigenous heritage. The Techialoyan documents attracted the attention of eighteenth- and nineteenth-century collectors and of present-day scholars. There are some fifty Techialoyans known today, early cases in the fabrication of evidence.

Robert Barlow was intimately familiar with the eighteenth-century Techialoyan forgeries; he knew that they were written on a rather thick and dark amate paper which easily separates and frays. Stephanie Wood, a prominent scholar, points out that late colonial *amate* was not up to the standards of skilled *amate* makers today, "whose fine products" are commonly available in tourist markets.[1]

So you never know. It's hard to believe that the Cardona is a falsification. Expert opinion and the sheer volume of work required for fake copies make that highly unlikely. But if a person such as Robert Barlow did not create the Codex Cardona from scratch, then speculation, even based on fragmentary information and evidence, might at least suggest a path that fraud might take. And if we want to run out such thoughts, Robert Barlow is as likely a candidate as anyone; no one was more qualified to produce the kind of work found in the Codex Cardona. Remember that despite the high-powered technology of PIXE analysis at the Crocker Laboratory, the radiocarbon tests and close scrutiny, experts in the field were unable to provide a definitive opinion on the Cardona's authenticity. This indicates that if Codex Cardona is indeed a fraud, the forgers knew what they were doing and were, moreover, deeply learned about the subjects recorded in the codex.

CHAPTER SIX

Sloan Ranger

If the world were good for nothing else, it is
a fine subject for speculation.

WILLIAM HAZLITT, *Characteristics*

 Faced with additional and contradictory evidence in trying
to piece together the Cardona's story, it was hard to know
what was real and what was not. It was hard to believe that
the Codex Cardona was a fraud; but, I had to confess, it *was*
suspect. If authentic, why all the secrecy? Why didn't the owner come forth
and tell where he'd gotten it, to do what he could to allay doubts? Presumably because there *wasn't* any plausible documentation? There wasn't even
any evidence for the existence of Alonzo Cardona y Villaviciosa, the Spanish
officer under whose direction the codex was allegedly produced. Research
trips to Mexican archives or, better, to the Archive of the Indies in Seville to
consult the voluminous records of the Spanish bureaucracy, already obsessively meticulous in the sixteenth century, might yield formal instructions
or at least mention a "Captain Cardona." No such figure had so far come to
light in the published work.

Another curious element in the problem of provenance was the frequent
mention of the owner's nationality. When the codex was offered to Sotheby's
in London, and again to the Getty and Stanford, Thomas Schwarz stated
that the owner was "an English gentleman resident in London"; the Getty
was told that he was "a gentleman of Hispanic descent resident in England."
A skeptic would immediately assume that representing the owner as British
was done precisely to deflect suspicions of a Mexican selling Mexican cultural patrimony abroad, aiming to circumvent the restrictions governing

the sale of an artifact from its country of origin. When I asked Nicholas Olsberg about this, he commented wryly that, for the Getty, "it would have been more convenient if the owner were British rather than Mexican."

On the other hand, you could take Schwarz's representation at face value: the codex's owner really was a British resident. In that case, how does a sixteenth-century Mexican codex get to London? And into the hands of "an English gentleman"? Here too were many possible stories; how was I to discover the right one? At the same time, my friend David, who had exhibited sporadic interest in the Cardona business until now, had gotten his teeth in the rag and was calling me frequently to discuss new hypotheses. His enthusiasms could be quite overwhelming, and lately I'd been feeling like a cockleshell in the wake of a heavily armed man-of-war. He insisted on coming up for a weekend and suggested a walk in the hills behind the house.

We did have a good long walk while David talked. By the time we got back there was a smoky, autumnal chill in the air. Inside, Alex had built a fire in the living room stove. After a bit the talk turned to my most recent conversations with the people at Stanford, which I hadn't told David about, and the lingering doubts about the Cardona's authenticity. We worked our way back into the free-floating, imagined reconstruction of possible scenarios of how the Cardona might have come into existence if it were not really an authentic sixteenth-century codex, and how it could have ended up in Britain.

"So," David began, picking up the thread we'd dropped some time ago, "Robert Barlow and his team of young tlahcuilos decide not just to reproduce a few pages of native documents for the popular education project Barlow was engaged in, but to undertake a larger work which eventually turns out to be the Codex Cardona? Isn't that right? Sometimes people do things just because they can. Maybe they got so caught up in making such real-looking copies of native documents that the more they made, the better they were, and Barlow ended up orchestrating the larger project."

"But what's the motive?" I asked. "And how does the Cardona end up in Britain after the war?"

"Well, let's imagine an Englishman posted in Mexico City just after the war as cultural attaché. Let's call him Evelyn, like Evelyn Waugh, the writer, or maybe Evelyn Russell. Or better, Russell Waugh. No that's idiotic. It's funny how the name makes a difference."

"I like Kenneth," I said. "Kenneth Bell."

He's fortyish, tall, affable, cultivated, and weak, from one of those mid-nineteenth-century Victorian industrial families but now with only a tiny inheritance, sliding down the social scale. Father in the Foreign Office. Maybe there's a baronet and a big house in the past. Anyway, he's acquired an interest in Mexican antiquities. Maybe he saw the Lord Kingsborough reproductions as a boy and then later, in Paris, the collections at the Musée de l'Homme or even the original Codex Mendoza at the Bodleian Library at Oxford, where, say, he studied classics. He's married to Julia McCrone, a plain and abrupt woman rather like Margaret Thatcher without the charm. Her coarse, hardworking, inventive father had made a fortune raising the German fleet scuttled at Scapa Flow and selling it for scrap iron and eventually raised himself into the Scottish gentry. Julia and Kenneth's marriage is the usual trade-off between new money, lots of it, and an older pedigree. It's not that they loved each other: he needed money, was available and not a great catch in any case. He gets minor assignments as a clerk in the Foreign Office, two years in the Cameroons, somewhere else, Paris for a year, then Mexico.

"Is that true?" Alex looked up from her newspaper. "I mean about the German fleet? Scapa Flow comes up in crossword puzzles."

"Yeah, I think in 1919. Scapa Flow is a harbor way up in Scotland."

"Anyway," I went on, "perhaps Julia has the money and keeps it under tight rein."

"She thinks the Mexican appointment is a demotion," David put in, "and hated Mexico even before she saw it."

A not entirely implausible scenario began to emerge.

In the early years of their marriage, Julia liked to show Kenneth off at parties in London, but his social ease, interest in pictures and books, his arty friends—all things she felt uncomfortable with—began to grate. After all, she's supporting him, paying for all this, while he spreads his charm around and is getting all the strokes. Besides, not long after the wedding he becomes indifferent to her crusty manner, so that by the time they get to Mexico, the marriage has wound down to impatience, irritation, and frosty resentment on her part, and a distant, trapped, helpless acquiescence on his.

We paused to mull this over.

"Okay," I said, "let's get them to Mexico."

So they get into the social-intellectual whirl. Remember this is Mexico in the late forties: Miguel Alemán and all the new money, new books and movies,

Rivera and Orozco and Siqueiros, those big modern stone-and-glass houses in Acapulco like in *Where the Air Is Clear*.

"Carlos Fuentes, *La región más transparente*," David corrected. He didn't read Spanish-language books in translation out of high principle.

"Okay. So there are diplomatic receptions up in Lomas, appearances at cultural centers, openings, lectures."

"It's just a matter of time," David added, "until Kenneth is introduced to Robert Barlow."

"Exactly. Remember that Colston mentioned that Barlow had done some of the dialogue for that Tyrone Power movie, so he's certainly not just a pith-helmet anthro but moves in the arts and film crowd."

And Kenneth, after all, actually *is* interested in ancient Mexico and knows something about it. So they meet.

Now Barlow. He's, say, just thirty. Brilliant, sensitive, a bit reclusive, or better yet dedicated to his work—he'd have to be to publish all those things before turning thirty-three. They meet. Barlow invites Kenneth to his office in the Indigenous Institute; Kenneth takes Barlow to lunch at Prendes. A mutual friend invites Ken and Julia along with Barlow for weekends in Cuernavaca.

"Remember how it was in the fifties?" I asked David, who had also lived in Mexico in the fifties. "I used to go down there myself. A great place, warm, tropical. I had this girlfriend, María Elena . . ."

So we have Barlow and Kenneth sprawled out in white linen in wicker chairs on a cool-tiled patio. There are thick, uneven, whitewashed walls, bougainvillea spilling down. Overhead Casablanca fans slowly revolve, all the clichés. Servants come and go silently, bringing cinnamon-flavored coffee and *pan dulce*. Barlow and Kenneth talk about Malcolm Lowry and the Mexican writers and about the fascinating explorations in Monte Albán and Palenque and about their common interest in ancient Mexico, about Tenochtitlán and Tlatelolco and the city's collapse in 1521. Barlow, of course, knows everything about this subject and talks about it in a most engaging way. In a matter of weeks, they're fast friends.

"Better yet," David said, "they fall in love. Let's say that Barlow was a little ambiguous in that area."

"Better yet, but where do we go with that?"

Well, they fall in love. And for the first time in their tormented, suppressed existences, they see the possibilities of a full life. All they need is money. Barlow lives in a bare-bones third-floor flat in Azcapotzalco, of all places, and if Kenneth peels off, there won't be anything coming from Julia!

We went on for a bit, but the fantasy tailed off. It was time for supper.

In early October I drove down to San Francisco, and David came up from Santa Cruz to meet me at the Palace of the Legion of Honor, practically the only place in the city where you can find a parking place. We sat on a bench looking across the bay to Marin, the Golden Gate Bridge on our right, the pounding of the surf below, gulls wheeling in the onshore breeze. A gorgeous late-autumn day.

"Maybe," I began, moving on to the inevitable subject, "as strange as it seems, there might have been something to that business we spun out about Barlow and the Englishman. At least it's an alternative path for how a Mexican codex that no one had previously heard of got to England."

We thought about this for a bit, tried some scenarios, couldn't get the story going, got up from the bench, walked over to the formidable equestrian bronze of El Cid, and wandered back to the bench. I wanted to tell David about the conversation I had with Enrique Florescano two weeks ago in Mexico City on a stopover on the way back from Chile. "I had a long lunch with Enrique and his wife Alejandra Moreno Toscano," I began, "in their house in the new section of Mexico out on the old Toluca road."

Enrique and Alejandra are both very well known scholars at the center of Mexican intellectual life. Enrique was for a number of years the director of the National Institute of History and Anthropology (INAH, the organization that is in charge of the great Museum of Anthropology in Mexico City, all of Mexico's archaeological sites, and a treasure trove of early documents and codices). I wanted to find out whether they'd come across anything, or had heard of, a painted book like the one I described at some length as the Codex Cardona. It occurred to me that the same book might be known by a different name in Mexico.

"They were incredulous." Enrique said it had to be false, otherwise "we'd know about it. It's hard to keep a secret like that for nearly five hundred years." We ran down a list of other specialists in Mexico, but as far as Enrique and Alejandra knew, nothing like the Codex Cardona was known in Mexico.

"That's worth knowing," David said. "If anyone knows the universe of codices and colonial documents, it's Florescano."

I had another glass of a decent Baja California red before I casually asked them both if people still remembered Robert Barlow and what kind of a reputation he presently had. Without a word, Enrique rose from the table, motioned me into his library—which is really remarkable—and showed me, as proof of Barlow's continued recognition, seven volumes of his recently reedited papers and articles. Enrique pointed out that Barlow was a real presence in Mexico in the 1940s, still remembered and admired today. Enrique mentioned, but didn't elaborate on, his "unfortunate end."

"Let's get back to the business of Barlow and, what do we call him, Kenneth?" I said.

Maybe, I thought, I could write all this up as a kind of Mexican academic tragedy set in the forties. Barlow alone is worth a short story, quite apart from the Cardona. With retirement coming up I was thinking of other projects to keep me alive.

I prodded David. "You had Barlow and Kenneth—Kenneth Bell—falling in love."

"Yes, they fall in love, for the first time. Physical, mental, emotional harmony. But no money."

"Or at least not enough to support the life Kenneth led with Julia," I said.

Besides, Kenneth would have told Barlow that it would be all over with Julia if she found out. And what can he possibly do to earn a living? Nothing; charm only goes so far. He has no skills, and there's nothing coming from his family. They lost it all after the Great War, in the twenties. For that matter, Kenneth must have shuddered at the thought of Barlow's bare-bones place, where they'd gone a couple of afternoons. I doubt that Kenneth was prepared to live a "Woolworth life," even for love.

"I've got it," David said.

Barlow thinks about his workshop, which has *some* money at least, from the Instituto Indígena, and he certainly would have got some grants. We might imagine five or six boys—*tlahcuilos*—in the shop making these scrolls and copies of Aztec and colonial codices and documents that look like the real thing. Tourists out at the pyramids at Teotihuacan eat them up. But that's small change.

"But, wait, wait! What are you thinking about? It doesn't make sense that he'd betray his life's work."

"But he's torn beyond measure by this passion for Kenneth."

"Yeah, I like it," David said. "This whole thing is beginning to convince me."

"Maybe we can have Barlow lying on a cot in his disorderly library in Azcapotzalco. The tormented relationship with Kenneth, who now leads a double existence, continues. It's unbearable."

"Sex and longing," David said. "The planet would be a hell of a lot better off if a really Intelligent Designer had backed off about 30 percent on the sex drive he handed out. Just think: far fewer people, no Trojan War, Monica might not have thonged Bill, he might not have responded, and so on."

Julia and Kenneth appear in the society pages of *Excelsior*. There are invitations by President Alemán to parties in Acapulco; new art openings, a retrospective of Edward Weston's photographs, the gaudy and expensive life in the postwar boom. Curiously, Kenneth's happiness has drawn Julia closer to him, and against all odds, she becomes pregnant; now she's more inclined to hand over a bit more—but not much more—of old McCrone's hard-earned fortune to pay for Kenneth's ever-more-immodest expenses, which now include folio sheets of *amate*, special vegetable inks and brilliant paints free of mineral traces that might spook skeptical buyers of what will become, Kenneth and Barlow hope, a beautiful, unique, and extremely high-priced painted book for the world antiquities trade.

"That's good," David said.

Now we could imagine Barlow in the workshop. He sketches out a plan, drawn from his own profound knowledge of the Valley of Mexico and its people, for his talented and highly trained *tlahcuilos*. He finds a couple of older guys, maybe former history students or teachers, who hang around archives reading old documents like they were newspapers. Some of them can even write in perfect sixteenth-century paleography. There are manuals like the Millares Carlo that would have helped.

The painters and scribes, working together, start with a few pages. They wet and bleach the *amate* with water from Xochimilco, still a lake in Barlow's day, to raise the saline content a bit, more or less how it was at the time of the conquest. At first the idea was to produce a single book of twelve or fifteen pages. But as the work unfolds, Barlow's vision widens. I'll never do this again, he swears in self-disgust, so to hell with it, why not an extraordinary work? An utterly unusual, unique codex. I'll make a pun and name it for the Aztec's glyph, the cactus in the foundation of Tenochtitlán. Cardus. The Cardona. The Codex Cardona.

"So that's the Codex Cardona," David says.

We got up from the bench and walked in silence through the eucalyptus grove north of the Legion of Honor's museum.

"Why don't you just write a fictional story and forget about the real codex," David said finally. "That is, if you don't end up finding it. Maybe the one we've invented is the one most people will think is real. That would be something, wouldn't it?"

"No, no," I said. "The thing is, after I saw the Cardona that day at the Crocker Lab, I wanted, and still want, to write a true story. I don't do fiction. I don't know how to write fiction. I might be no great shakes as a historian, but nonfiction, serious nonfiction, is the only thing I know."

David wouldn't let up. He thought we should continue to spin out our story of how the Codex Cardona got from wherever it was—say, from Barlow's workshop—to "the English gentleman of Hispanic descent," or the gentleman of Hispanic descent resident in London, and then to Sotheby's.

"I mean, that's a real question, and you haven't turned up a single idea about that one. Let's go down to one of those old Basque places in North Beach, on Broadway. We can continue the story there. How a Mexican codex gets to London is a question you—well, we—have to resolve. A bit of brainstorming might at least set out some possibilities."

We had a thick soup to start, clams in garlic-soaked rice, a plate of roast lamb with potatoes, sautéed garbanzo beans with more garlic in a separate bowl, lettuce and tomato salad, a carafe of red table wine, an apple torte and espresso. During the meal, the talk strayed from the Codex Cardona.

"Let's walk down to the Tosca bar if you want to play out the Barlow business," I suggested. "But I don't want to hit the interstate too late."

The haunting flute solo from Gluck's *Orpheus and Eurydice* was coming out of the old-style jukebox as we walked past the long bar and mirror. There was a quiet table in the back.

"All right," I began, "so the Cardona is finished, or nearly finished. It's taken nearly two years."

Julia is invited to accompany some embassy women to another opening and luncheon. Kenneth isn't sure where. He dreads the thought of an afternoon in the Azcapotzalco flat and mentions to Barlow that they haven't been back to the lovely Las Mañanitas in Cuernavaca since they first met. "Do you remember?" Kenneth asks Barlow. "It was so sweet."

They decide to go down on Saturday. Kenneth gets the Embassy car without "that *dreadful* Mexican driver." He touches Barlow's arm. "I know, I *do* know, that you—well, both of us—have been under tremendous strain. I just want to stretch out with you under the jacarandas, bathe in the pool, have a proper gin and tonic, go to bed, be together the way we can be. Julia, thank God, is away somewhere for the weekend."

Barlow, as we say now, is stressed out. He's looking forward to the rest and quiet. He believes he loves Kenneth, but he's also tormented not only by this love which, God knows, would be a scandal among his colleagues but also by guilt over the work that is being finished that very day in his workshop.

On the other hand, Barlow tells himself, he hasn't really done anything wrong. The scribes and painters have simply done what they've been doing since he trained them. Nothing wrong with that. The Instituto Indígena *supported*, in fact *encouraged*, the project. If a rich collector or library—or even the Peabody at Harvard, where he'd studied—wants to buy the recently made Cardona, fine. No one is saying that it's original or sixteenth century. And if we're successful, there will be money for the institute.

But of course Barlow knows better, and his torment returns. I'm betraying my colleagues, he tells himself, corrupting my own work and self-respect, throwing caution to the winds for a weekend indulging the flesh.

Julia's luncheon, of course, as the god of coincidence would have it, takes place precisely at Las Mañanitas. From the terrace, she sees Barlow and her husband come from the pool. They walk through the garden past the peacocks strutting on the lawn, past Zúñiga's massive bronze female figures, and enter their room. Julia hesitates until the insult and the outrage settle into her brain. She demands their room key from a terrified concierge and bursts in.

"Not an ennobling scene," as she will describe it years later to a confidante in London.

Julia and Kenneth return separately that night to the house in San Angel. She demands that they leave Mexico—she'd always hated it—and return immediately to Camsie House in Scotland. "I will not let this stand. The shame. The *horror*. You will inform the ambassador that you are no longer able to carry out your job. You don't do anything anyway. Invent a reason. I'll take poor Ian and leave in a matter of days. You can pack on your own and return to Camsie. Appearances will be kept up for Ian's sake. But *you* will never be forgiven."

The same night, May 21, 1951, around 2:00 a.m., according to the federal police report, Robert Barlow lay down in his narrow cot in the third-floor flat in Azcapotzalco and shot himself in the head with a .38 revolver, a gift from his former stepfather as protection against "barbarous Mexico." A week later his mother flew to Mexico, gathered his ashes from distraught friends, and scattered them under an *ahuehuete* tree in El Desierto de los Leones, a tranquil convent garden on the road west out of Mexico-Tenochtitlán.

"This last part," I told David, "is true. It's another thing my grad student found in the Barlow papers at the University of the Americas in Puebla."

What next? What does Kenneth do? His first thought is to protect himself; the second is to get his hands on the codex. He takes a taxi to the workshop, finds a grieving José Jiménez, Barlow's longtime collaborator in the Educación Pública project and main illustrator of the Cardona, guarding the *taller*—the workshop. Kenneth persuades him to carefully wrap the document, now over four hundred pages long, in kraft paper and tie it together with—what's that Yucatán cord? Henequen? No, sisal. He takes it home, packs it among his and Julia's most valuable possessions, and sends them via the British Foreign Office's courier to Camsie House outside Edinburgh. No problem with customs; the book is safely inside the diplomatic pouch.

"You're persuading me," David said. "Go on."

Okay. We fast-forward to the late 1970s. Both Julia and Kenneth have kicked the bucket. Ian, Ian *McCrone*, since Julia insisted that Kenneth's family name be dropped, is now thirty-three, the same age as Barlow when he shot himself in Mexico. Ian dropped out of Harrow, went down to London as a late teen, got into drugs and bad, even dangerous, company. In his twenties, after his mama's death, he becomes a kind of Sloan Ranger in swinging London and blows most of his inheritance.

"What's a Sloan Ranger?" David asked.

"The too-rich, stylish, upscale British yuppie who hung around in the fashionable bars and boutiques near Sloan Square in Knightsbridge, I think."

"Anyway," I went on, "so pretty much down and out, Ian goes up to the house outside Edinburgh, where he hasn't been since Julia and Kenneth died."

He's rummaging around in the big downstairs library, and tucked away behind broad shelves he finds, in a fiberboard case tied with frayed cord, an old, exotic painted book. Ian suddenly recalls that once his mother had mentioned that she and Kenneth had brought a peculiar book from Mexico. He had also been struck at the time by his mother's extremely distasteful way of talking about it, which perhaps jogs his memory now.

Ian had seen enough precious things to know that here was something really unusual and probably valuable. And he'd made enough connections in London to know where to go for an opinion on the book's worth on the antiquities market. He finds a reputable agent to offer the book, described on the title page in the sixteenth-century Spanish hand as the Codex Cardona, to Sotheby's on consignment for £6.7 million, around $8 million at that time.

Sotheby's, as we know, was suspicious and turned it down. But Ian finds a more aggressive agent in America to offer the Cardona to the Getty and later to Stanford. Ian McCrone, then, is the "English gentleman resident in London" described by Thomas Schwarz in the Crocker Lab. And no one in the world except José Jiménez—if he's still alive—knows this incredible history of the Cardona. Unless, of course, you count the two of us.

Well, David and I mused as we left the Tosca, it doesn't have to be Robert Barlow; but it's the kind of scenario that *could* explain a post-1945 forgery. And really, who knew the world the Codex Cardona describes better than Barlow?

CHAPTER SEVEN

Nights in the Gardens of Coyoacán

Tonatiuh had a friend, or perhaps he said that "he *knew*
someone—I'm not sure—but in any case, there was a person,
a person who preferred to remain *anonymous* (Tonatiuh emphasized the word)," who had something that he was sure
would absolutely interest the Getty.

The speculations about Robert Barlow, however improbable
they seemed at the time, did serve to widen the exploratory
screen and open up other hypothetical trajectories; but it
was hard to know where to go from there. I hadn't forgotten Thomas Schwarz, who had represented the Codex Cardona's owner (or
owners, or forgers, or thieves) at the Crocker Lab, but I'd had no luck finding him. Colston had lost track, but after hearing his story, I tried again to
find Schwarz, who was clearly a key player if he could be found and if he'd
talk.

Colston had given me the address of a bookstore at 738 South Bristol in
Los Angeles where he'd once met Schwarz. But the letter I wrote to Schwarz
was returned: "Not at This Address." On later trips to Los Angeles, thinking that he might have a new store, I searched the phone books and looked
through the lists for book dealers, rare books, and antiquities, both in L.A.
itself and in surrounding cities such as Santa Barbara and San Diego; I also
searched the Internet and scanned through the many telephone books that
the library collects for other American cities. The Stanford people—I rang
Jim Fox—had lost contact long ago. Schwarz had vanished. Perhaps he'd
died.

Nicholas Olsberg, of course, had dealt with Schwarz in the Getty negotiations, so I turned again to him. Olsberg, who was retired, had recently

moved from Santa Barbara to Arizona, but I found a forwarding number. He was friendly and helpful.

"Yes," he said, "as you know, Tom Schwarz worked with us at the Getty on several projects. He's quite well known and comes from an intellectual Jewish background in Vienna, a very respectable book dealer."

Olsberg gave me an address, more recent than the one I had for Schwarz on Bristol Street in Westwood. Olsberg thought that Schwarz had gotten married and moved out of his mother's house to Santa Monica. Olsberg also had an unlisted number for Schwarz, which he gave me. A call brought an irate, even violent, male reply. "No, you jerk. No Thomas Schwarz at this number." The slam rang in my ears. Whoever had answered didn't sound at all like an intellectual Jewish antiquities dealer.

But a couple of weeks later I got a fortuitous break. I had gone to visit some friends in Marin, and after lunch, browsing the shops on Mill Valley's main boutique street, I saw a poster in a bookstore announcing the opening of

> Thomas Schwarz
> Antiquities, Rare Books, Maps, Documents
> 7 Melody Lane

Under my very nose, right here, of all the unexpected places, in Mill Valley, just a hop and a skip north of San Francisco.

I rang Schwarz's number the next day from my office. "You won't remember me," I said, "but we met almost twenty years ago at the Crocker Lab. You had a Mexican codex you were trying to sell to Stanford." Schwarz paused, seemed surprised, then became affable, charming. I'm sure he didn't remember me, but he certainly remembered the codex. We agreed to meet the following Tuesday, May 24, 2005.

I drove my Honda up the narrow, twisting road to 7 Melody Lane, Mill Valley, in marvelous Marin, the wealthiest county in the United States, where the three floors of a large wood house sprawled down the hillside. Mr. Schwarz was just setting up shop, and there were piles of books and unpacked trunks in a large, sparsely furnished room that looked out onto a hillside of shedding eucalyptus and tangled madrone. Not another house in sight.

Schwarz was heavier than I'd remembered him from the Crocker Lab, with a smooth, plump body and hairless head, sensual lips, big teeth, and a wide smile. I reminded him of our previous meeting. He looked at me closely and feigned memory. In the course of our get-acquainted chitchat, he mentioned something about Berkeley, and we discovered that we had both been there during the same years in the mid-1960s: he as an undergraduate in European history, I in grad school. The phone rang; he heaved himself to his feet, said something about a son, talked in a hushed voice, and came back to the living room. We chatted a bit about his move to Marin. "Because of my former wife and son," he said.

Schwarz was guarded but interested that I was pursuing the story of the Cardona. I brought up memories of our first meeting, of the three Stanford anthropologists, the cold lab itself, and of course the Cardona, to try to establish a common ground. He offered a plain cup of tea with no saucer or milk, and we gradually eased into his association with the Getty and how he had come to offer them the codex. I was, to say the least, enormously interested in all of this and in how he had gotten to know about the Cardona in the first place. He made clear that his association with the Getty was over.

The experience with the Getty and then with Stanford must still have burned in his brain because as we talked he revealed a fantastic recall of detail. It must have been his biggest potential deal ever, and I later learned that he'd spent $20,000 of his own money for trips back and forth to Mexico, which probably made his memory more acute. He wasn't sure what to make of me or of my interest in the codex, or just what kind of story I had in mind to write. For that matter, neither did I. "Are you thinking of a history of the Cardona, or is this fiction, a novel?" he asked.

Not surprisingly, Schwarz was hesitant at first, holding his cards as close as possible to his broad vest. He must have been wondering how he would come across in my story. Nevertheless, as the sun broke through the morning mist, he warmed up and became quite voluble. I had to remember that his association with the codex had happened quite a while ago; many of the principals were probably dead or retired.

As a rare books and antiquities dealer in Los Angeles, Schwarz told me, he was asked by a woman — he didn't provide the name — to help the Getty develop its collection, primarily in pre-Columbian and colonial Mesoamerican materials. He was subsequently offered all-expenses-paid journeys to Mexico and Guatemala to seek out collectors and dealers. This was two or three years before he offered the Cardona to the Getty, around 1982–83. Happily for Schwarz, his preparation for the buying trips to Mexico coincided with an international exposition of rare books and antiquities held at the Ambassador Hotel in Los Angeles.

Schwarz went around the exposition with several colleagues in the trade, including Howard Karno, a Los Angeles dealer who specialized in Latin American material. Schwarz noticed and was fascinated by a "flamboyant, charismatic, impressive Mexican who practically filled the exhibition hall of the Ambassador with his passionate energy." On one occasion they stood side by side looking at a luxury edition of the Kingsborough reproductions, but they did not introduce themselves. Karno had good connections with the world of Mesoamerican manuscripts and gave Schwarz the names of important dealers and collectors in Mexico City.

Shortly after the exposition, Schwarz made his first trip to Mexico and quickly made useful connections. During one such appointment, on a spring evening with the jasmine in bloom and crimson bougainvillea everywhere, he rang the bell of a high, adobe-walled house on Francisco Sosa Street in the charming district of Coyoacán.

From Schwarz's description, I could imagine the scene. The owner of the house, an important *coleccionista*, welcomed Schwarz into his library. To his surprise, the dashing man he had seen at the Ambassador Hotel was standing by the fireplace. This was Tonatiuh Gutiérrez, a former medal-winning swimmer, professor of economics at the National University of Mexico, promoter of the popular arts, and expert in pre-Columbian dance and dress. Gutiérrez was married to an equally accomplished woman named Electra López Mcompradé, the daughter of Spanish republican exiles to Mexico in 1939. Both moved in fashionable intellectual circles in Mexico. Tonatiuh—the name means "the Sun" in Nahuatl—was the son of a high government official during the heady pro-indigenous years of President Lázaro Cárdenas, when many Mexican children were given Aztec names. Indeed, Cárdenas himself initiated the popularity of such names, calling his own son Cuauhtémoc in memory of the last independent Aztec ruler.

The owner of the house welcomed Schwarz, invited him to browse while he continued his conversation with Tonatiuh, displaying a number of early-sixteenth-century maps of Mexico and the Caribbean. Tonatiuh was looking ahead to the interest that the five hundredth anniversary of Columbus's landfall would generate. After examining the maps, Tonatiuh, whose English was excellent, turned to Schwarz, and they discussed colonial books, maps, and other documents that the *coleccionista* brought out. With Tonatiuh translating, the three men talked about their general interest and about the present market for antiquities. Schwarz cautiously revealed his commission from the Getty to the two men, a bit of information that—although they wouldn't have shown it—must have quickened their pulses.

A frail, white-haired Indian servant padded into the library to light the fire and bring a warming cognac. Spring nights at seven thousand feet are chilly. Later, leaving together, Schwarz and Tonatiuh walked through the patio garden and into the Mexican night, finding kinship in the discussion of old books.

After describing his meeting with Tonatiuh, Schwarz went to the kitchen of his Mill Valley house and, bumping the door jamb, brought out a plain white-china teapot, now cold, and a couple of hard brownies on a paper plate.

"My people came from Austria; Vienna, actually," he said, "which of course has a lot of history and culture, but that night in Mexico I really felt like I was in the presence of an ancient, fascinating civilization. Have you spent any time in that country?"

As Schwarz told me about the meeting in Coyoacán and his sense of wonder about being in Mexico, it called up my long-ago student memories of Mexican nights and the dramatic charm of that country. I was touched by the innocence of Schwarz's discoveries, a quality I suppose that all of us have when we first visit a new country. I knew that Schwarz couldn't have known that just down the street from where he stood with Tonatiuh that night, Diego Rivera and Frida Kahlo had been married a half century before in a no-holds-barred celebration in which Diego had shot the phonograph with his .45 revolver. And a few blocks farther along, eleven years after that wedding, a Stalinist agent had sunk a climbing ax into Leon Trotsky's large-domed head. Not, of course, that this had anything to do with the codex; it's just that I felt as possessive about Mexico then as I do now about the Cardona.

Putting Schwarz into a taxi on Francisco Sosa Street, Tonatiuh invited him at a later date to come to his house (not far away, in fact, just around the corner in Belisario Domínguez Street) to meet his wife, perhaps also some other interested people, and to examine a number of items that Tonatiuh thought might interest the Getty. During the next several days, Tonatiuh introduced Schwarz to the treasures of colonial Mexico. He had his driver take them through the streets of the Centro Histórico, to the Zócalo, to the newly renovated Franz Mayer Museum and the Church of Santo Domingo, to the convent where Sor Juana Inés de la Cruz wrote her precocious poetry, and then back to his house for late suppers with Electra and their friends.

After two or three such days and nights, Schwarz said, Tonatiuh presented him with what seemed like a remarkable opportunity. Tonatiuh said that he had a friend, or perhaps he said that "he *knew* someone—I'm not sure—but in any case, there was a person, a person who preferred to remain *anonymous* (Tonatiuh emphasized the word)," who had something that he was sure would absolutely interest the Getty. Tonatiuh said he wasn't exaggerating, that the item was unusual, unique, in fact, and extremely valuable. But he couldn't show it to Schwarz in Mexico.

In fact, Schwarz told me, "I never actually *saw* the Cardona in Mexico."

Tonatiuh then told Schwarz that if the Getty showed a serious interest in the piece, he would find a way to bring the codex to California.

Schwarz returned to Los Angeles and immediately got in touch with Nicholas Olsberg, head of the Getty's Special Collections. Olsberg expressed a guarded interest and told Schwarz that if the item could be brought to California, "then of course we would have a good look."

"I gave Tonatiuh the green light," Schwarz told me, "and a few weeks later, one day in late March or April 1985—I have my notes somewhere—Tonatiuh came to my house (I was living in Santa Monica then) with a tightly wrapped package in a fiber suitcase. It was, of course, the Mexican painted book, the Codex Cardona."

Schwarz said he leafed through some of the four hundred or so folios, and then he and Tonatiuh drove to a Wells Fargo bank near the Getty to rent an oversized safe-deposit box for the codex. "To my complete surprise—and I confess that it made me nervous—there was no documentation, no receipts for me to sign, just an unambiguous and even stern admonition that the codex was to be well taken care of." Schwarz added that he felt a slight sense of menace in the remark. Tonatiuh left that evening. Schwarz wasn't sure where he was going or, for that matter, from where he had brought the Cardona to Los Angeles.

So what had I learned? I'd already known that Thomas Schwarz had turned up with a Mexican codex in Los Angeles and offered it to Olsberg at the Getty. Now I had traced the Cardona back to Tonatiuh Gutiérrez, an intermediary in Mexico City. Moreover, I also knew that at more or less the same time (1982 or 1983) that Schwarz was talking about a valuable "piece" with

Tonatiuh Gutiérrez in Coyoacán, someone was negotiating with Sotheby's to take the Codex Cardona on consignment in London and was showing the Cardona around at the International Congress of Americanists in Manchester. For whatever the reason, the codex's owner or his agent was aggressively promoting the Cardona in those years. Schwarz's revelations raised other questions. Had Tonatiuh also represented the Cardona at Sotheby's? Why this particular flurry of activity during these years? Nor did these revelations resolve the question of ownership; instead they seemed to complicate the earlier claim about the codex's provenance. I'd been led to believe that the owner was a "Hispanic gentleman resident in London." Had Tonatiuh actually come from London to Los Angeles that morning? Did Tonatiuh Gutiérrez personally know the owner, or was he just another go-between? Was he a friend or accomplice of the architect Gutiérrez Esquivel, who had written the peculiar letter in the Getty file? Since I had no direct evidence, it was impossible to know.

When I aired these questions with Schwarz in Mill Valley, he was evasive and, moreover, had some bad news. Tonatiuh was dead. He had passed away some three years earlier. This made me acknowledge that many of the players in the story were getting old—including me. I had to get cracking. Tonatiuh's widow, Electra, would surely know something. I put her on my list of people to try to see in Mexico.

Then, too, I had to keep in mind that Schwarz, an experienced dealer in rare books and antiquities, may not have been wholly candid, or at least not unnecessarily forthcoming, with either the Getty or Stanford—or with me. He had clearly been fascinated, if not enchanted, by the sophisticated Tonatiuh and the attractive and accomplished Electra López Mompradé, not to mention with the glamor and sophistication of the high-end Mexican book and antiquities trade, and probably even now hadn't ruled out further dealings on his own. Schwarz was certain that with the Cardona he'd had a tiger by the tail; and, as he told me, he had invested a substantial sum of his own money in the effort to sell the Cardona to the Getty. He saw no connection between Tonatiuh Gutiérrez and the other Gutiérrez—the architect, Gutiérrez Esquivel—whose letter was in the Getty file. Perhaps Schwarz was unaware of the letter; Olsberg had no reason to show it to the dealer.

As I prepared to thank Schwarz for his time and the tea and leave, I was able to confirm that many of the features of the Cardona story that I'd heard before were present in his account. Tonatiuh insisted that the codex's owner must remain anonymous; there was no discussion of provenance or any proper documentation. Schwarz said he'd asked Tonatiuh how a 450-year-old codex could lie hidden from public view until the 1980s, but his query was politely ignored.

Schwarz's account did make clear, however, that there was not only doubt about the Cardona's authenticity—whether it's really sixteenth century, a later copy, or a complete falsification—but also some concern about carrying a Mexican antiquity across an international frontier. Didn't customs officials have questions? After all, there were international agreements, the 1970 UNESCO convention, signed by Mexico in 1972—but not by the United States until 1983—whose purpose was to prevent the importation and exportation and illegal transfer of patrimonial property, including most specifically archeological and ethnological artifacts. If the Codex Cardona was not an "ethnological artifact," what was it? The Cardona was not only an ethnological artifact but a *Mexican* artifact, and any Mexican carrying an item like the Cardona across the border into the United States would invite extreme curiosity, to say the least.

The looting or theft of artifacts and their subsequent sale to museums or private collectors are part of a very old story that began long before Lord Elgin hauled the Parthenon's marbles off to the British Museum and scattered the rest in the foyer of his Broomhall estate in Scotland. International conventions have not prevented illicit acquisitions, but such transactions open the possibility of litigation, forced restitution, and embarrassing publicity for both the buyer and seller—or the museum or looter. If any institution is aware of that, the Getty certainly is.

Tonatiuh, I noticed, had been careful not to show Schwarz the Cardona in *Mexico*; but, of course, it may not have been there. When he appeared in Los Angeles with the codex in hand, Schwarz told me that he had no idea where Tonatiuh had come from—Mexico, Spain, London, or elsewhere. Tonatiuh had brushed off Schwarz's concern about whether he'd had "a good flight." Schwarz told me that since he'd met and dealt with Tonatiuh in Mexico, he had assumed that the codex had been flown from Mexico City to Tijuana and then carried across the border to San Diego and to the Getty. When I asked how it might have passed through customs, Schwarz dismissed the problem as no big deal: "They have a way of getting these things done."

Schwarz walked me to my car. "I hope you'll keep in touch about the Cardona. I have some contacts with big-money collectors. Not Bill Gates, but people in that range. If the codex turns out to be authentic, something might be done there. You never know what people go for."

I thanked Schwarz for the story about Tonatiuh and Electra.

"Tonatiuh died three or four years ago," he repeated, "but I kept in touch with Electra and call her from time to time. I can ask if she remembers the codex and if there's any news. In fact, maybe I could see if she'd like to talk with you."

"I'd really appreciate that," I said, shaking his plump, slightly damp hand.

After a half dozen telephoned reminders that I would very much like to talk with Electra López Mompradé, Schwarz had not called back. I later learned that she had moved to Spain from Mexico shortly after Tonatiuh's death. That meant that she was actually in Spain during the two years when Schwarz claimed he was keeping in touch with her in Mexico.

CHAPTER EIGHT

A Mysterious Affidavit

Fernando Blanco Ladrón de Guevara, declares . . . that he believes he
remembers, that among the papers and documents that belonged to the
illustrious Señor don Felipe de Neve y Padilla, governor of California . . .
there was a book dealing with Mexico City, handwritten, of a good size,
with illustrations, from approximately the sixteenth century.

 The Codex Cardona was still out of sight, but my talk with
Thomas Schwarz had brought a new player, Tonatiuh Gutiérrez, into view, adding new and intriguing information.
Mulling over my speculations about Robert Barlow, any
thought that the codex might be a recent falsification still seemed possible
but remote. Sometimes the whole quest for the Cardona seems bizarre to
me; perhaps I had let my enthusiasm run ahead of my common sense. Who
knew? Perhaps a wealthy owner, a legitimate collector, had wanted to test
the market and, when faced with what might have seemed frivolous objections and quibbles about authenticity, had simply withdrawn the codex and
locked the case in the library. No mystery, no drama, no big deal. Was there
really a good story here? And could I write it? Like poor Keats, I had "fears
that I may cease to be / Before my pen has glean'd my teeming brain."

I rang Colston to see if he'd heard anything; he hadn't, but he remained
fascinated by the case. I exchanged courteous e-mails with Nicholas Olsberg, searched library catalogs in every way I knew, checked the usual
sources. Coming through Mexico, returning from a jaunt to Chile, I had
lunch again with Enrique Florescano, but he'd heard nothing. Few leaves
turn in museums, publishing, or the high-end book and antiquities trade
in Mexico without Enrique being informed. Besides, he'd be chagrined to
learn that something as exotic as the Cardona might be floating around
the world and a gringo, not him, would be the one to break the story. A

new, comprehensive book, *Codices*, by the renowned Mexican Miguel León-Portilla, the world's foremost general specialist on the subject, had just appeared in 2003 with no reference, no mention, of a Codex Cardona or a *Relación Cardona*. At an international conference in San Francisco in 1992, I exchanged a few words with a UCLA professor who had no doubt that he himself was the world's foremost specialist on codices. He indicated that if *he* hadn't heard about the Cardona, "it was either unimportant or a cheap fraud."

Back in my office, I was happily surprised to find a letter from Jim Fox at Stanford. It was something I hadn't expected because just two weeks had gone by since our last meeting in September 2005. I arranged a date and drove down to see him. This time he was waiting for me in the parking lot. He seemed pleased to see me, and we walked up to his office, chatting amiably. Out front a cheerful young woman — one of his daughters, it turned out — was working at a computer. Entering Fox's office, I was struck by the profusion of electronic gear, scanners, computers, elaborate cameras, everything neatly ordered. I remembered how cluttered it had been on my last visit and presumed that his daughter had straightened things up. Some family pictures were propped up on his desk, and some attractive rice-paper rubbings made from Maya stelae hung on the wall.

Fox talked a bit about his daughter; he told me again that he had seven children, even asked about my years in Chile. Maybe Fox had mellowed, or perhaps he'd cracked the Maya glyphs, something several different scholars claim to have done since the 1950s. In any case, he was no longer reserved. He asked how much further I'd gotten with the Cardona. "You must know more about that codex than anyone else in the world by now; well, it *is* a fascinating story." He said that he'd contacted me because in cleaning up his office, or rather when his daughter had cleaned up his office, they'd found a few things: one that he'd been reluctant to give me, and another that he'd overlooked when we met two weeks ago.

"But then I remembered that it has been at least twenty years since we met at the Crocker Lab — how time flies! Anyway, I doubt that anyone, except maybe you, has any interest in these things but you're welcome to them."

The first item was a small batch of thirty-two color slides that his colleague, one of the anthropologists present at the Crocker Lab that day, had secretly taken of a few folios of the Cardona with a hand-held camera. That surprised me; I remembered that Schwarz had insisted on no copying.

"I still feel a bit guilty handing them over to you. They're not very good quality; George snapped the pictures in a rush, on the sly, at random. The agent, Tom Schwarz, kept the codex in a Wells Fargo strongbox here on campus and gave us only an hour at a time—literally only an hour—alone with it."

"You'll see two or three slides of that incredible map of Mexico-Tenochtitlán," Fox continued, "which didn't come out very well because George couldn't get the entire thing in, and there are other shots of completely original material dealing with the huge Albarradón sea wall project—well, breakwater, really—showing the techniques of pile driving from floating rafts, and there are charming pictures of Aztec women patting out and baking tortillas on a *comal* in flat-bottomed launches to supply the workers. So there are those. Then there are some loose papers, copies of the radio-carbon tests, some letters about who was to pay for the Crocker Lab examination, and so on."

"But then there's this," Fox said. "I don't know if it will interest you, but because of the doubts we'd raised about authenticity and particularly about the murky ownership question, Schwarz, toward the end of our negotiations, produced this affidavit."

Fox handed me a photocopy of a three-page document, in Spanish, with the signature and official stamp of one Antonio Fernández-Golfin Aparicio, "notary of the illustrious College of Madrid, resident in this capital city." The text, in my translation, goes like this:

In Madrid, the eleventh of January, 1985, there appeared before me, don Fernando Blanco Ladrón de Guevara, *carnet* number DNI, 346.918, married, a lawyer, and a resident in Madrid with a home address in the Calle Santiago Bernabeu, number 8, who declares, to whom it may concern, that he believes he remembers that among the papers and documents that belonged to the illustrious Señor don Felipe de Neve y Padilla, governor of California and founder of the city of Los Angeles, California, that in this family archive, there was a book dealing with Mexico City, handwritten, of a good size, with illustrations, from approximately the sixteenth century.

This book must have been sold by my father, the illustrious Señor, don José María Blanco White Quintana de Neve, to a certain Baron von Schultzenberg-León in approximately 1928.

Our family had contacts with Señor Schultzenberg-León, a resident of Switzerland, until the beginning of our civil war and then, with the global conflagration of World War II, we failed to have any notice of him, not knowing where or when nor how he died.

I have read the present document to the person who has appeared before me and he approves it. He signed the document in my presence.

Signed, Notario de Madrid, Antonio Fernández-Golfin Aparicio, Calle Maldonado 28, Madrid 28006. Teléfonos 403–4650; 403–4708.

"Where in the world," I asked Fox, "did this document come from; I mean before Schwarz got it?" Taken at face value, and if "a book, dealing with Mexico City, handwritten of a good size, with illustrations, from approximately the sixteenth century," could possibly be the Cardona, then, I thought, Fernando Blanco's testimony could illuminate the dark trail of the codex's past by establishing antecedents back at least to the late eighteenth century and by offering rather more plausible evidence than my Barlow speculation to explain how the codex might have gotten to the "Hispanic gentleman resident in London" who was supposed to be its owner. And if the notarized document were legitimate, the case for a post-1945 antecedent would, of course, evaporate.

"Schwarz came up with it," Fox recalled, "after the Crocker Lab tests had come in without definitive proof of authenticity, at a time when our Special Collections people had become very nervous about the possibility of fraud. But I don't know how either Schwarz or the owner got it. Schwarz wasn't telling."

Fox reminded me that he had dealt with Schwarz over quite a few months.

"He was traveling back and forth to L.A., and on one of those trips, toward the end, he brought this copy of the document. It was a little strange to us that he could produce it just when we were pressing him on the provenance question rather than have included it in the original file."

Tonatiuh, I thought, must have had a hand in this, since he served as a courier between Schwarz and the Cardona's owner during the Getty negotiations. Perhaps Tonatiuh knew this family in Spain, or perhaps he knew the notary and leaned on him to produce the document. Then I remembered that Electra, or her Spanish father, had come to Mexico as part of the republican exodus after 1939. She might be involved. On the other hand, the document could simply be legitimate. It's not easy to get a forged notarized affidavit; notaries in the Hispanic world are extremely formal.

The notarized document did fit the story given to Olsberg two years before at the Getty. He'd been told that a "Hispanic family in England after the war" had acquired the codex. Schwarz had muddled this—maybe deliberately, maybe he didn't know for sure—telling both Olsberg and Fox that the codex had been sold by Baron von Schultzenberg-León and later acquired either by "an Englishman resident in London" or by "a person of Hispanic descent resident in London." Lots of different versions.

A presumptive sale by Baron Schultzenberg-León to a buyer in Britain also fit the pattern of the large trade in manuscripts, paintings, and artifacts that opened up when the international barriers were lowered after 1950. Lots of art and artifacts that the Nazis had appropriated during the war also came on the market at that time. Maybe don José María Blanco White Quintana de Neve—a high-powered name—was an aristocratic fascist and, seeing the approach of the Spanish civil war, wanted to bail out, needed cash, sold the "good-sized Mexican book with illustrations" to his friend the Baron von Schultzenberg-León, and, and . . . but no, there was no point in spinning out this wild notion with no evidence and now with so many other uncertainties in the air.

In any event, whether false or not, don Fernando's testimony is certainly hedged about with qualifications and abounds with the subjunctive mood. He "believes he remembers" (*cree recordar*) that his father "must have sold" (*debio ser vendido*) the book to a Baron von Schultzenberg-León. Anyone would also notice that don Fernando doesn't refer to "the Cardona" or to a "codex" but to a "book with illustrations." This, however, is not surprising or worrisome, since if the codex did come into the family from Felipe Neve in the eighteenth century, the term "codex" was not yet common at the time, and the label "Cardona" may not have been used until the document was offered for sale at Sotheby's.

Nevertheless the notarized document that Fox now revealed was potentially important, had to be examined, and maybe even represented a breakthrough in my story. Certainly it raised a lot of questions. The first was how did the owner of the Cardona, or his agent—say Tonatiuh—know in 1985 that the Blanco or Blanco White family had anything to do with an "illustrated Mexican book"? And if the owner did know of these legitimizing antecedents, then why didn't he present them immediately to Sotheby's or to the Getty as part of the sale package rather than wait until Stanford insisted on evidence of provenance? Put another way, who persuaded Señor Fernando Blanco Ladrón de Guevara to appear in a Madrid notary's office on January

11, 1985, and bear evidence, however hedged about with evasive language, on the Codex Cardona's history? Schwarz had been silent on this matter, though he had most likely been handed the affidavit by Tonatiuh during one of his shuttles to California.

Now, with the notarized document in hand—assuming for the moment that it *was* a legitimate notarial document—would I be able to find don Fernando Blanco or his descendants? Who was his father, this José María Blanco White Quintana de Neve, who had found the book? His name, of course, suggested a family relationship, even if distant, to don Felipe Neve, the "governor of California and founder of the city of Los Angeles." And what about Baron von Schultzenberg-León, the Swiss-Spaniard who is supposed to have bought the codex from José María Blanco, kept it in Switzerland through the years of the Spanish civil war and World War II, and then sold it to someone in England? Did the present owner acquire the Cardona from that "someone" or from someone else? Once again, I wished I knew. In the notarized document, Fernando Blanco says that his family had contact with von Schultzenberg-León until the beginning of the civil war and then seems to indicate that he died perhaps shortly afterward.

About these and many other questions I could only speculate. But since the story of the Cardona had neither beginning nor end—I didn't know where it came from or even where it was at the moment—I thought that I may as well backtrack, as best I could, to its origin, a procedure that historians often think explains things.

I took the new material Fox had given me back to my office and began to look into the family of don Fernando Blanco Ladrón de Guevara. I first rang the telephone number indicated in the notarial document for the notary, Señor Antonio Fernández-Golfin Aparicio, in Madrid. "No señor, there is no *oficina de notarías* at this number." Nor did a Fernando Blanco Ladrón de Guevara appear in the Madrid phone book, available in the university library. But of course lots of people, particularly important or wealthy people, there as here, have unlisted numbers; and then too we all die, go on to the other shore.

Light bulb over the head—I'm a lingering premodern, slow to take up new devices—I turned to Google. The Blanco Whites appeared in a flood of URLS.

CHAPTER NINE

Seville and the Firestone

Quien no ha visto Sevilla
No ha visto Maravilla.

ancient refrain

 As you enter the barrio Santa Cruz in Seville by turning right off Mateos Gago onto Calle Jamerdana and just before reaching the Plaza de los Venerables, an elegant plaque, perhaps two feet by two, is set into one of the thick white walls in this charming district. The barrio of Santa Cruz was once—before 1492—the principal Jewish sector in the city. In decorative black script surrounded by a border of linked green leaves on glazed white tile, the plaque reads:

EN ESTA CASA CALLE JAMERDANA
NACIO EL 22 DE JULIO DE 1775
JOSE MARIA BLANCO WHITE.
La ciudad de Sevilla agradece una vida dedicada
A combatir la intolerancia

The walls in this district are not marked with graffiti or covered by posters and advertisements. In places you can extend your arms and touch both sides of the narrow way. The thick, sweet scent of jasmine seems to descend like an invisible mist, and in the second-story balconies, clay pots holding geraniums hang on wire frames, a tribute to the ancient Arab adaptation to scarce water in arid lands.

I had walked up Calle Jamerdana many times during the six months I lived in the barrio Santa Cruz some thirty years ago. Some nights, before the suffocating heat of the tourist season came, in the little *plazuelas* in the quarter, I was lucky enough to hear local youths singing, only for themselves, the wailing African sounds of the Andalusian *cante jondo* accompanied by a flamenco guitar. On the Plaza de los Venerables, the Hostería Laurel set out wobbly wooden tables and chairs, and there were bars next door where you could have a manzanilla or a small glass of draft beer and paper cones filled with fried calamar.

Because of that time in Seville, reading in the great Archive of the Indies during the day and exploring the city by night, many details, such as the plaque dedicated to this man with the curious name, were engraved on my brain. Everything glows with a lasting brilliance when you're young and well-accompanied in such a place as Seville in the spring. So when I found several pages of hits for José María Blanco White on Google, it was easy to imagine the ancestral mansion with its dark, cool library, its heavy curtains drawn against the summer heat, in the Calle Jamerdana. I felt I already had my heart invested in this part of my inquiry.

A great many papers, diaries, letters, and official documents of both powerful and humble families decay in forgotten attics or are simply tossed out as members die or move; or they rest uncataloged in obscure archives. Had it not been for Internet search engines, I could never have imagined that a large part of the Blanco White papers had been collected by Princeton University. They were there because of José María Blanco White, the man named on the memorial plaque, who in the course of his active, questing life during the turbulent years of the Napoleonic Wars and the struggles for independence in the United States and Latin America had been a rebellious Catholic priest in Spain and later emigrated to Britain to become a well-known poet and political figure in Oxford. Not the person I was looking for; but fortunately, the collectors of his family's papers have cast their net wide, so their catch begins with the foundation of the Blanco White family in the late eighteenth century and continues into the 1930s.

Since the notarized document produced by Thomas Schwarz in the Stanford negotiations indicated that a member of this family—indeed, the namesake of the man on the plaque—had the Cardona in 1928, I could hardly wait to get my hands on the eighteen bundles in Princeton University's Special Collections.

My daughter Rebecca lives in Brooklyn. She was happy to accompany me— she suggested it—and on a brisk late October morning in 2005 we made our way through the early morning rush in Penn Station and were on our way to Princeton. On the train I told her at some length about what I'd been doing—always risky, since I've learned that our offspring don't have a lot of patience for being talked at by their parents, or at least by this parent. But Rebecca seemed keen to work with me, which made me happier than I can tell. I'd arranged from California that the eighteen bundles in the Firestone Library be pulled and ready for our examination.

Our aim was to backtrack from the presumed ownership of the Cardona by José María Blanco White Quintana de Neve in 1928 as far as the trail led into the past. The notarial document said that the "book with illustrations" had originally been found among "the objects and documents" belonging to the "illustrious Señor don Felipe de Neve, governor of California and founder of the city of Los Angeles, California." So this connection, if it could be established, would be most interesting because it would demonstrate the colonial Mexican origin of the Cardona and perhaps confirm the validity of the notarial document.

I had found a good modern biography of Neve, which outlined his career beginning as a young officer posted to New Spain (the colonial term for Mexico) in the 1760s.[1] I brought the book to Brooklyn, and Rebecca had a good look at it. She had several questions that we mulled over on the way down to Princeton Junction. The main one was: Could we show that Felipe Neve, during his service in Mexico, somehow acquired and passed on to the Blanco White family in Seville the illustrated book that came to be known as the Codex Cardona?

The biography gave the basic facts. Felipe de Neve y Padilla was born in Bailén (province of Jaén) into the old aristocracy of Andalusia in 1727. His father was a captain in the Spanish cavalry; his mother came from the distinguished family of Padilla y Castilla. A distant ancestor, Justino de Neve (1625–85), has a street in Seville named for him.

As an army cadet, young Felipe was named to the Royal Bodyguards at nineteen and commissioned as a lieutenant in the Royal Army in 1749. Fifteen years later, leaving his wife in Spain—they had no children—he sailed to New Spain with the contingent led by the powerful crown inspector general José de Gálvez (for whom Galveston, Texas, is named). A year later, in 1765, Neve was appointed assistant to the Marquis de Rubi to form the Provincial Calvary of Querétaro.

Felipe Neve's service in Mexico was part of the reforms undertaken by European monarchs throughout the Atlantic world provoked by the growing imperial competition among England, France, and Spain for the American colonies after the Peace of Paris ended the French and Indian War in 1763. Neve rose rapidly through the ranks of the Bourbon military bureaucracy to become governor of the Provincias Internas of northern Mexico and also governor of the "Two Californias" — Lower and Upper California. In the course of this work, he founded the city of Los Angeles and the presidio of Santa Bárbara, California. Neve died on the march in northern Mexico in 1784.

Now, just when and how, during his illustrious career in Mexico, Felipe Neve might have acquired a book about Mexico City, "handwritten, from approximately the sixteenth century, of a good size with illustrations," was a challenging question. I had to remind Rebecca that Fernando Blanco — the man in the 1985 affidavit — had remembered, or more or less remembered, that the "illustrated book" had been found in the 1920s by one José María Blanco White Quintana de Neve among the possessions of his ancestor "the illustrious don Felipe Neve."

Rebecca and I agreed: If the illustrated book about Mexico City *was* found in the Blanco White family archive, "among the objects that had belonged to Felipe Neve," then presumably Neve had to have acquired it during his years in Mexico and then in one way or another had passed it on to some member of the Blanco White family in Seville. Rebecca could certainly see that here we were entering the realm of slender evidence and conjecture, and she gave me the raised eyebrow I remembered from her teenage years. But the thing is — I came up with one of my old admonitions to undergraduates — sometimes you have to work like a lute maker, guided by touch and feel, rather than with the precision of a drill press. At this bit of fatherly wisdom, Rebecca looked out the window.

In the back of the biography were appendixes dealing with Neve's military record. After his successful service with the Marquis de Rubi, Neve was put in charge of expelling the Jesuit order from the important silver-mining center of Zacatecas. This operation was part of a hemisphere-wide Bourbon policy that led to the banishment of Jesuit priests from all Spanish and Portuguese possessions in the New World and the subsequent outlawing of the Jesuit order in 1772. Neve, like crown officials throughout the Spanish empire, including even the Philippines, was given sealed orders to proceed to Jesuit *colegios* and missions on the morning of June 25, 1767, seize their property, arrest the individual priests, and send them immediately on the road to exile and secularization in the Papal States in northern Italy. The biography said that Neve carried out these orders with characteristic alacrity.

About this time Rebecca's cell phone rang. "That was Quentin," she said. "He *can* pick up Lily after work."

I explained to her how in the eighteenth-century Americas, the members of the Jesuit order, drawn from nearly all the countries of western Christendom, were the most educated, intellectual members of Spanish, French, and Portuguese colonial society. Coming out to America in the late sixteenth century, they were first posted to the far edge of the "rim of Christendom," that is, to the Amazon headwaters, the far south of Chile, the Mexican northwest, and Baja California, among other missions. But above all they soon became devoted to educating the white Creole elite in the impressive Jesuit *colegios* (the term describes a secondary school for elite boys) established in nearly all the principal cities in the Spanish and Portuguese empire. The Jesuits were also collectors of books and manuscripts. They became fascinated by the indigenous past of Mexico and Peru and were the authors of enduring works on these subjects.

I was conscious of sounding like a textbook, but what the hell. Rebecca seemed to be bearing up admirably.

On the morning of June 25, Neve and a small detachment of Spanish soldiers under his command would have burst in on the Jesuit complex in Zacatecas—one of the richer sites of this world—which included the *colegio*, church, library, living quarters, silver mines, and rural haciendas. Almost immediately the good fathers of the Black Robe—"Didn't you see that great movie *Black Robe*?" I asked Rebecca—taking with them only their immediate possessions, were packed off to Vera Cruz to await passage to the Papal States.

Neve took everything having to do with the *colegio* under his personal control and served as general administrator of Jesuit properties in Zacatecas for seven years. The Spanish crown later sold the rural properties and mines at public auction.

It doesn't require a great leap of the imagination to see Felipe Neve rifling through the confiscated Jesuit documents and papers in the *colegio* library to find this elaborate painted book and claim it for himself. The biography makes clear that he was, by all accounts, an educated, cultivated man.

If, in fact, Neve acquired the book "of a good size with illustrations" in Mexico (how else would it have ended up among his "objects, papers, and books" in Seville?), it makes sense that he got it from the Jesuits. The inventory of confiscated Jesuit property assembled by crown officials dwells on their extensive rural and urban properties, on the baroque opulence of church and *colegio*, on the silver, gold, and pearl-inlaid items for the liturgical services, and makes a general mention of stacks of books and documents in libraries. But unfortunately the description of the library holdings, its manuscripts and papers, is not itemized.

The problem is that there is no concrete evidence anywhere that I know that the Jesuits had actually acquired a Mexican painted book during their two centuries of intellectual work in Mexico. Was it in the library or study of the Zacatecas *colegio* on June 25, 1767? We don't know, but it's certainly possible.

No one knows, at least I didn't know, what had happened to the Codex Cardona after the painters and scribes went home — let's hope with at least a pat on the back — four centuries ago, in 1554. For that matter, I don't know where the codex is now. But Pagden, in his report for Sotheby's, included the tantalizing bit of information that a Jesuit priest, Francisco Calderón, had in his possession a painted book with two important early-sixteenth-century maps with "figures and explanations," which the Jesuit father believed important enough to show to the viceroy of Mexico in 1630.

This rudimentary description *could* apply to the Cardona; it certainly would not describe the few other *Relaciones* of that time, all of which are more modest in scope. Could this document, if it were indeed the Cardona, have ended up in Zacatecas in 1767? We have Fernando Blanco Ladrón de Guevara's statement that he "believed he remembered that he had seen" something like the Cardona among Felipe Neve's "objects and documents" in his father's house in Seville in the late 1920s. So if this is true, in what other way could the Cardona have gotten there except through inheritance from Felipe Neve, the "illustrious ancestor"?

We turned to Neve's career path after the successful expulsion of the Jesuits. After administering the former Jesuit properties in Zacatecas, he was appointed governor of the Two Californias in 1774. His dirt-floored headquarters were in Loreto, Baja California. He soon moved to equally rustic quarters to Monterey in Upper California and is credited with founding the city of Los Angeles. In 1783 he was promoted to brigadier, named comandante general of the Provincias Internas, in effect of the entire Mexican northwest with its capital at Arispe, Coahuila. On August 21 of the following year, on the march to Chihuahua, he fell ill and died on the road. A few days earlier he had dictated his last will and testament.

"I ordered Neve's will from the archive in Seville," I told Rebecca, "it should be in California when I return."

We got off the New Jersey Transit line at Princeton Junction, took the rickety shuttle to the end of the line, and walked to the library. It was farther than we thought, and I got a little out of breath. The librarians of the Firestone's Special Collections were prim and precise. They showed us the Rolodex file of the Blanco White collection, gave us pencils and special paper to prevent theft, and asked for my briefcase and Rebecca's purse. In the hexagonal reading room, with a large oil painting of John Foster Dulles on the wall, dappled autumn sunlight filtered through the tall windows. The quiet tap-tap of the librarian's keyboard was the only sound. An African American woman with a picture of her pet poodle as a screen saver kept watch over the room.

What would we find? My heart quickened as the first bundles were brought to our desk. Somewhere in the papers would we find an inventory, perhaps, or an offhand remark in correspondence about a Mexican painted book or "un viejo documento" that "my uncle Felipe had sent from Mexico"? That might be too much to expect.

We leafed through lists of expenses, personal letters, clips of old newspapers, funeral costs — the funeral of Felipe Neve's niece Gertrudis had cost $4,812.80, no small amount in 1819. We learned that Gertrudis's mother, Teresa, had brought a dowry in jewelry worth 15,000 pesos to her feckless husband, Francisco Crespo.

Although the eighteenth-century and nineteenth-century hand is easy to read, it was slow going. We worked our way through boxes 5, 15, 16, 17, 18, and 19, which seemed from the index the most promising. From the marriage, baptism, and funeral documents, we pieced together a direct line of descent linking the eighteenth-century governor of California with the apparent owner of the Cardona in 1928. This required clearing away the near-intractable tangle of intermarried family names in this provincial upper-class society, where matronymics and patronymics double back and repeat, where each generation's sons are inevitably named Fernando or José María. The genealogy giving the direct line of descent went like this:

Neve's possessions were divided into eighths: four-eighths left to his wife, Nicolasa Pereira y Soria (who, unknown to Neve, had died while he was in Mexico). A perfunctory one-eighth was left to his nephew, Lope de Ollaquí y Neve, "who possesses rich estates and needs nothing from me," and the remainder went to his favorite and beloved sister Teresa Neve, who lived separated, abandoned by her husband, Francisco Crespo.

Teresa had three children: Antonio, who died in New Orleans in 1783; Josefa, who joined a convent; and—here was the connection to the Blanco White family—a third daughter, Gertrudis Crespo de Neve, who married William White, a successful merchant and Irish consul in Seville. After marrying into the Crespo-Neve family, William White translated his name to Guillermo Blanco, keeping, however, the ancestral White, hence the family "Blanco White." Gertrudis Crespo and Guillermo Blanco White were the parents of the well-known poet whose name I'd seen on the memorial plaque in the Calle Jamerdana in Seville, and the reason Princeton had collected his family papers in the first place.

The marriage of Gertrudis and Guillermo Blanco White produced two sons, José María Blanco White and Fernando Blanco White (1786–1849), who established a military career in Spain. Fernando's *primogénito*—firstborn son—was José María Blanco White y Ollaquí (1823–60), who in turn was the father of Mariano Blanco White y Valdenebro (1857–1934), who married Maria de la Salud Quintana. This couple produced a single son, José María Blanco White Quintana de Neve, who was—according to his own son—the person who "must have" sold "a book dealing with Mexico City, handwritten, of a good size, with illustrations," to Baron von Schultzenberg-León around 1928.

This succession makes it possible and even likely that if our eighteenth-century governor, Felipe Neve, acquired the Mexican illustrated book in Mexico (where else would he have acquired it?) and shipped it to Seville among his other possessions (what else would he have done with it?), it would have been passed down through his favorite niece's direct heirs. If so, the notarized statement that a Mexican painted book was discovered in the 1920s by the person in the direct line of descent, José María Blanco White Quintana de Neve, makes sense. Nor is it surprising that the painted book may have lain quietly out of sight in the ancestral library, its curtains pulled against the Sevillian heat, unknown and undisturbed by the Blanco White family for nearly a century and a half. I confess that I was conscious of subjecting the evidence to extreme torture. But archives and historical documents rarely yield without pressure—and imagination.

Time had flown by. We'd been in the Firestone Library all day under the stern gaze of Mr. Dulles's portrait. This was the first time I'd ever sat side by side with Rebecca in such affectionate harmony. I didn't know which was more thrilling: reading the Blanco White papers or doing it with my beloved daughter. We asked the woman with the poodle screen saver to gather up the bundles and walked across campus to catch the last train back to Manhattan.

We got back to Brooklyn late, taking a cab from Penn Station, and I returned to California on the midnight Jet Blue flight. The next day I found a FedEx package propped against my office door. At first I couldn't bear to open the slick red, white, and blue envelope for fear of finding nothing. But inside was Felipe Neve's last will and testament, seventy-two photocopied pages from the Archive of the Indies in Seville. Here was my chance to find the evidence we hadn't found at the Firestone Library. I tried to imagine Felipe Neve on his deathbed in a remote town in northern Mexico, dictating to his aide-de-camp a list of his worldly possessions. Might there be an explicit mention of "a painted book" that "I acquired in the course of my duties for my king"?

Felipe Neve's will commends him to God, invokes several saints and the Virgin of Remedios and the Macarena, and lists obligations to debtors, the money owed to him, some personal effects of silver and gold plate, expensive buckles, an "English gold watch," and several other minor possessions stored in a nearby garrison, which were to be sold by his executors. Then he turns to a general mention of "objects" and "movable goods," including furniture, arms, and *libros* and *papeles*. But no explicit mention of a painted book with illustrations or maps.

I flipped impatiently to the back pages of the will, hoping against hope that more talk of chests and *posesiones* would include the specific mention of a painted book. There was an anexo to the will with more brief mention of "muebles i libros" (furnishings and books) and even the mention of "un grueso volumen de pergamino con mapas del reyno de México de regular tamaño" (a thick volume of parchment with maps of the kingdom of Mexico of good size), but nothing clearly resembling a Mexican painted book, especially one with hundreds of paintings and unforgettable maps.

Could this "thick volume of parchment" in Neve's will be the Codex Cardona? If it were, why no mention of the many painted illustrations of good size? The Cardona is definitely oversized. Neve would have made a special effort to acquire such a book, and you'd think it would have occupied a special place in his will. Let's also remember that the "Mexican book with illustrations" that José María is said to have found "among his illustrious ancestor's papers" in 1928 was no insignificant or ordinary book. It attracted the attention of Baron von Schultzenberg-León, was long remembered by Fernando Blanco Ladrón de Guevara (in 1985), and later was a prized possession of that unidentified "Hispanic family in England." It certainly should have been noticed by Felipe Neve.

On the other hand, the Blanco White papers *do* show—if Neve acquired the Codex Cardona in Mexico—exactly how it could have been passed through a direct line of descent from Neve to his heir, José María Blanco White Quintana de Neve, in the 1920s.

But this leads to another and even more interesting issue. The author of the notarial affidavit presented to Stanford had to possess thorough knowledge of the Felipe Neve-Blanco White family history and its hereditary lines of descent. Indeed, he would have to know what we had just discovered in the family archive!

I was not able to verify that a don Fernando Blanco Ladrón de Guevara actually appeared in Madrid that January day in 1985, but that doesn't mean he didn't. It's also true that the affidavit does not explicitly say that the "handwritten book from approximately the sixteenth century of good size with illustrations" is the Codex Cardona. It leaves that to the reader's imagination. But it's clear that the intention of whoever presented the affidavit to Stanford was to lay out a plausible trail designed to show anyone doubtful about the provenance of the codex evidence of its authenticity. It's almost as if the person who produced the affidavit anticipated a future sleuth in the Firestone Library.

It's possible—as in many things related to the Cardona—that the affidavit is a fake. At the same time the person who presented it to Stanford, as well as the man who dictated the affidavit to the Madrid notary, may be completely innocent in spirit and intention. In that case, perhaps Felipe Neve might have acquired the Cardona in Mexico, and it was later found by his direct descendant in 1928 in Seville.

If a fake, who were the clever and informed authors of this deception? For the present, the issue remains unresolved.

CHAPTER TEN

Christie's of New York

The Codex Cardona devotes several pages and vivid illustrations to a second indigenous woman, María Axixina (or Achichina or Chichina), who was accused of gathering weapons for an apparent anti-Spanish conspiracy; she was discovered and hanged, and her house was burned.

 In mid-June 1999, Professor Stephanie Wood, an ethnohistorian at the University of Oregon, called to tell me that seven months earlier she had been asked to provide an opinion on a sixteenth-century Mexican document. She had been invited to do so by Christopher Coover, a rare book and manuscript expert (and future vice president) of Christie's, the famed auction house in New York City. Coover briefly described the codex and indicated that Christie's would pay air travel and all expenses in New York, plus a handsome honorarium. The document was the Codex Cardona.

In the course of her evaluation and reflections about the nature of the codex, Professor Wood got in touch with a number of other specialists in her field, including Stephen Colston, a fellow ethnohistorian we've already met, who had briefly consulted with her during his own evaluation of the Cardona for the Getty in 1985. Colston suggested that she get in touch with me.

We compared notes. I gave her an updated account of my on-again, off-again pursuit of the codex with doubt and frustrations at every turn in my efforts to discover the codex's provenance and its present owner and location; obviously I was more than intrigued by this new turn of events. I filled in more detail about the codex's appearance at Sotheby's, the Getty, and Stanford—which she didn't know about until she'd talked with Colston—and about the previous questions of ink and paper and the radiocarbon tests. Stephanie Wood was understandably guarded in her account, as was Christie's, in the information Coover provided to her. He pointed out that the negotiations were very "hush-hush."

I had no doubt that the Codex Cardona had circulated and was talked about among a closed circle of private collectors and rare book dealers in Mexico and elsewhere, but as far as I knew there was no public notice of the codex, no offer by its owner or owners, for sale or consignment, since it was last seen at the Getty Museum and Stanford fourteen years earlier, in 1985. Now, someone—she was not told who—was asking Christie's to take the codex to be sold for "several million dollars" (she was never given the precise figure) while the owner, in Coover's words, still "preferred to remain anonymous."

And then, as silently as it had appeared, the codex disappeared. After five months of evaluation, Christie's turned down the offer for consignment in May 1999 and the codex was carried off—by whom, Christopher Coover was not telling.

I was in Chile for most of the four or five years after our initial exchange in 1999, and during that time, Wood and I exchanged occasional e-mails. Once Christie's had washed its hands of the Cardona, she added more detail to her opinion of the Cardona and eventually sent me a copy of her report. We shared gossip, reported new (if scant) information, tried to piece together the order of events in an elusive chronology, and speculated on provenance and destiny—that is, where the codex came from and who presently had it. But these questions were unresolved.

In his initial request in 1998, Christopher Coover asked Stephanie Wood to pay special attention to the question of possible fraudulence or forgery; for among her professional attributes Professor Wood is a specialist in the controversial and suspect "Techialoyan Codices" that have already been discussed. For this purpose she chose to take a linguistic approach to the Cardona manuscript, focusing on vocabulary, as she tried to determine whether the scribes and painters were native Nahuatl speakers and the degree to which they might have absorbed the postconquest Hispanic culture in just two or three decades.

Stephanie was able to spend only a few days at Christie's in New York and upon her return to Oregon, she got in touch with three experts in sixteenth-century paleography and linguistics to ascertain whether Italianate, Portuguese, or Catalan influence might be detected in the text and to find evidence of a later, perhaps eighteenth-century, influence or even a more recent forgery. Christie's wanted a report in a matter of weeks; given the difficulties of the early-sixteenth-century hand, this was a formidable task. She finished the evaluation for Christie's working alone in a small cluttered room off the main offices in Manhattan, drafted the report, and sent it off in December.

"The Codex was fascinating and it's still a real mystery to me," she e-mailed. "Lots of contradictory information. I'm not sure I resolved anything for Christie's and I didn't know what they were going to do with it. In February or March 1999 I was told the consignment was looking positive. But then it was turned down in May—the whole background, the lack of documentation on provenance and ownership, was, in Coover's words, 'too murky.'"

She had received a bit of a clue from Colston. While "rummaging" through his old files (which, he said, had been moved several times and were in disarray), he'd come across a note made in July 1997, about a call from a certain Roberto Asaz. Señor Asaz had called from Mexico City claiming to be a rare book dealer who was checking on behalf of his colleague, a distinguished architect who did not speak English. Colston said that even though he had seen a letter in the Getty file from a "distinguished architect" called Guillermo Gutiérrez Esquivel, he hadn't put that name together with Asaz's colleague.

After completing her report for Christie's, Wood got in touch with specialists in the sixteenth-century hand in the United States and Spain who allayed some of her doubts. They pointed out that it is not unusual to find Portuguese, Catalan, and Genovese influence in early-sixteenth-century texts. The brown ink of the Cardona is less common than black but is nevertheless found in other Mexican manuscripts. As for *amate*, which troubled everyone who wrote evaluations for Sotheby's, the Getty, and Stanford, it's true that the Cardona's famous contemporaries, the Mendoza and Telleriano-Remensis, are on European paper. But a few others—the contemporary Codex Xólotl, for example—is on *amate*. And it turns out that in the mid-sixteenth century there was an *amate* paper mill in the town of Culhuacan, one of the places dealt with by the Cardona. During the course of our discussions, Wood mailed me a copy of her report to Christie's.

Like Pagden, Colston, Nicholson, and everyone else who has seen the Codex Cardona, Stephanie Wood was impressed by it, but also wary. The information given in the Codex Cardona," she wrote, "is wonderfully detailed and beautifully done. It would—if authentic—considerably enrich the picture we have of the first generation of colonial life following the Spanish invasion and seizure of power."

Professor Wood, unlike the other evaluators, seemed to have read almost all of the difficult text and gave a full description of the range and depth of this remarkable document. "The market city of Tlatelolco, in the northern part of Mexico-Tenochtitlán, is especially well represented in the Cardona. There is not only a description of the renowned market of Tlatelolco, which so impressed the first conquerors, but also fine coverage of the legendary Colegio de Santa Cruz, with a discussion of its famous instructors, Bernadino de Sahagún and Andrés de Olmos, and new information on lesser-known friars." Church construction in the capital is especially well detailed, as are the techniques used in the construction of the great flood wall directed by Viceroy Velasco. "I loved the wonderful illustrations of chinampa farming on the shores and lake islands," she remarks; "these are the famous 'floating gardens,' tourist attractions today."

There are maps and censuses of the lakeshore communities, material on land distribution, discussion of work and taxes, and an unusual painted illustration of how the common laborer's hard-earned coins were distributed along an extensive chain of hands all the way to the crown. There is graphic evidence of abuses by priests, the burning of other painted books, and the whipping of an Indian noble, as well as descriptions of salt making, fishing, flour milling, and bread making by the invaders (who insisted on wheat bread, not corn bread). We see textile production, the burning of cadavers in the wake of the first epidemics, and a portrait of another baptized and well-known Indian noble, don Juan Guzman Itztollínqui, governor of Coyoacán from 1526 to 1554, a detail that would support the sixteenth-century authenticity of the Cardona.

"The censuses of early Spaniards that accompany the maps are unusual if not unique," she continues in her report. "They show the scant number of Spaniards present in early Mexico, reveal the servants they'd brought from Cuba, and refer to slaves from Guinea and the Canary Islands. There are frequent remarks about Jews, Moors, Mozarabes, Flemings, and others that reflect the attitudes of the early postconquest era. There are references to mulattos and the first generation of mestizos and comments about the 'great scandal' caused by the presence of these 'bastards in the Spaniards' houses.'"

The architectural material in the Codex Cardona, Wood wrote, would be a boon to historical research. The functioning of the New World innovation of the open-air chapel that incorporated indigenous outdoor ceremonialism is beautifully illustrated in Libro A, on page 121 and elsewhere. There is a scene showing the construction of a church in Xochimilco. with two indigenous men holding up what appear to be the plans for the church and a friar explaining them to the master artisans. The early church architecture is abundantly shown here, with detailed drawings of houses and official buildings.

"But it's in cartography that the Codex Cardona makes its most stunning contributions. The map of Culhuacan contains, for instance, vague remnants of indigenous cartography (probably copied from an indigenous-authored map), including the glyph-like symbol of the crooked hill of Culhuacan and the swirling waters of the spring of 'Atochixco.' Sixteenth-century maps of the Valley of Mexico, and especially of the capital city, are rare and extremely valuable."

Wood noted, as mentioned before, that the Cardona's foldout map of Mexico-Tenochtitlán on four elephant folios (a contemporary of the Santa Cruz map, c. 1550, now in Uppsala), is the jewel of Sweden's National Museum of Ethnography. There is also a separately bound map of Coyoacán, which is actually the largest of the Cardona maps. This map has surprising detail, with references to houses of such prominent figures as doña Marina, also known as Malinche, the famous native guide and translator for the invading conquistadors. In the Cardona, Bernal Diaz del Castillo, the chronicler of the conquest, is said to still own his house in Coyoacán.

Wood also noticed "the painted sketches of the two women" mentioned earlier in Pagden's evaluation for Sotheby's. One, a doña María Bártola, is pictured sitting at a table actively writing. She is described in the text as the author of an account of Cortés's siege of Tenochtitlán. Doña María, obviously a baptized Mexican, is mentioned in the writings of Ixtlilxóchitl, but because her chronicle was apparently lost, she disappeared from memory. The Codex Cardona devotes several pages and vivid illustrations to a second indigenous woman, María Axixina (or Achichina or Chichina), who was accused of gathering weapons in an apparent anti-Spanish conspiracy; she was discovered and hanged, and her house was burned. One of the Cardona's illustrations shows her with accomplices carrying arrows; in another she's dangling from the scaffold with co-conspirators: "This kind of information is exceedingly rare, and rarer still in colonial history are images of women with quill or paintbrush."

The Cardona also surprisingly mentions the most illustrious female figure in Mexican history, the Virgin of Guadalupe, and associates her with the site of Tepeyac. "Some will see the mention of her," Wood points out, "as an indicator that the Cardona must date from the seventeenth century or later, since most scholars believe that the Virgin did not become much of a legend until after 1649. Still, there was local enthusiasm associated with a chapel devoted to Guadalupe on Tepeyac as early as 1550 and the scribes of the Cardona may have picked this up."

There are many other topics in the Cardona, including illustrations and texts dealing with the fateful encounter between Cortés and Moctezuma; Spanish parades that memorialize the conquest; portraits of Xólotl referred to as both a Chichimec and a Toltec lord; several illustrations of the 1324 founding of Tenochtitlán; paintings of the ancient nobility of Chalco, and so on. Some features of the codex are similar to those in other early Mexican codices, such as the "daily life" segments of its contemporary, the Codex Mendoza, and are not unlike some of the *Relaciones Geograficas* from the 1570s.

Yet the question remained. Is the Codex Cardona an authentic sixteenth-century "painted book" as the owner or his agent represented it to be? Or is it a later copy (perhaps from the eighteenth-century) of earlier documents? Or even an ingenious and exceedingly laborious post-1945 forgery? Wood's account, like previous evaluations, doesn't resolve these questions. She presents evidence for authenticity; still, there are doubts and red flags. "There are no official seals," she emphasized, "no elaborate rhetoric of introduction in the Cardona, that one might expect to find in a report to the Spanish king." She, like others, was troubled by the paper, which, she repeats, should be on European paper, not *amate*, given the codex's importance and date of compilation. Wood originally believed the orthography suggests that at least one scribe had an Italian or Latin education, as seen in such words as "mullieres" for "mujeres," "omes" for "hombres," "ínsula" for "isla," and so on.

During the four or five years following the news of the Cardona's appearance at Christie's, no new information came up on my screen. In my e-mail exchanges with Stephanie Wood she maintained her doubts about authenticity. Her many contacts in the scholarly world of Mexican ethnohistory were skeptical that a wholly unknown early colonial codex would come to light more than four centuries after its production.

She mentioned again the secrecy surrounding her evaluation at Christie's. No one would reveal either the name of the owner or the details regarding Christie's negotiations and subsequent rejection.

"I worked with Coover and also a woman named Hope Mayo, who I think has moved on," she wrote. "I recall now that Coover mentioned that the owner may have been a European or an Englishman, but it was all very hush-hush. Now that the Cardona has moved on and quite a few years have passed, they might talk with you. I have Coover's telephone and e-mail address. They were both terribly interested and also pretty skeptical about the Cardona."

On August 30, 2005, a few days after that e-mail, I rang Christopher Coover at Christie's and explained myself and my interest in the codex.

"No, I can't tell you who the owner was," he said with an edge of irritation, "our policy doesn't permit that."

We talked in general terms about the codex. When the talk faltered, I presented my question in another way.

"All right," I persisted, "let me run two names by you to see if they ring a bell. May I do that?" A hesitation, then cautious consent.

"Roberto Asaz?"

"No."

"Guillermo Gutiérrez Esquivel."

"I will tell you," he said, "that that's *not* the name we had."

Another pause. "But I will tell you this: you might want to talk with John Gloine, who, we were told, was a representative of the manuscript's owner, to ask whether you could arrange to see the codex. His telephone in London is 011 44 20 7233 2694. Good luck."

The next day I went to my office and called the number at a reasonable hour in London. I rang every twenty minutes or so for the next two hours. Busy. I repeated the effort for two or three days, calling at slightly different times: always busy. Finally, an adult male voice answered. I introduced myself and asked for Mr. John Gloine. "No," a stern voice replied ending in a shout, "NO, NO!" That was all.

Maybe it was a wrong number answered by an irate householder who had received several calls for a John Gloine. Sometime later, I rang again to find that the number had been disconnected. There wasn't a number in the London directories, no mention on the Internet, nothing. No John Gloine among the dealers in antiquities and rare books in Britain that I could find. If he existed, he wasn't visible.

After the brief conversation with Coover and the non-response from the "John Gloine" number, I ran the latest developments past my young colleague Andrés Reséndez over cappuccinos near my university office. He's a Mexican who studied at the Colegio de México and then at the University of Chicago, and had also worked with Clio, the big Televisa affiliate. Andrés is well connected, knows lots of people in the Mexican academic and artistic world, and has lots of Mexican gossip.

I'd kept Andrés up to date on my research. We both suspected that Gutiérrez Esquivel had something to do with the Cardona, maybe even was, or had been, its owner. He'd written that curious letter—not saying that he was the owner but recommending the Cardona to the Getty as a disinterested observer. But in my earlier conversations with Nicholas Olsberg, he too had an inkling that Gutiérrez Esquivel might be the owner or at least might know who the owner is. Whether Olsberg would ever tell, of course, is a separate matter.

"Why not see what a telephone call will turn up?" I said to Andrés; "there were two numbers in the letter that Gutiérrez Esquivel wrote for the Getty." Andrés could call, I suggested, thus putting an intermediary between Gutiérrez Esquivel and me. He could say that he was representing his colleague, a University of California professor who didn't speak Spanish but was interested in Mexican manuscripts, and particularly in something called the Codex Cardona.

We didn't think that Gutiérrez Esquivel would consider this threatening since we weren't customs officials or Interpol agents, for God's sake, but merely historians. In fact, we could say that we had found information about the Spanish antecedents of the codex that might interest him and wondered if, in turn, he knew where it might presently be found. We could also say that we'd talked to Stephen Colston, someone he might be familiar with from the Getty report.

Back in my office, Andrés rang the first number in Mexico City, presumably Gutiérrez Esquivel's house. There was a disconnect—out of service. We rang the second number. The call was answered by "Laura," apparently a secretary. Andrés asked Laura if she would be so kind as to connect him with El Señor Arquitecto, Guillermo Gutiérrez Esquivel, briefly explaining our general interest in Mexican manuscripts. "Don Guillermo," explained Laura, "is a very busy man and cannot come to the phone. If you leave your number I will pass on to him your requests."

We waited three or four days and called again. Laura repeated that the previous message had been passed on as the current one would be. But again there was no return call. A week later, we called a third time. Laura was annoyed. There would be no telephonic response. Why all the mystery? If the man had it and wanted to sell it, why not talk to an interested party? Or perhaps he'd sold it? Or maybe never had it?

CHAPTER ELEVEN

El Palacio del Marqués

"Víctor never goes to museums," she explained with
affectionate disapproval. "Gutiérrez is a *coleccionista*, and he's
restoring the hacienda as a place for his *colecciones*."

 In my younger days, after four years in the U.S. Air Force,
two of them in Morocco, I had gone to Mexico City for two
years to study economics. There I became fast friends with
two university students with whom I kept up over the years,
particularly Víctor—Víctor Lomelí. I traveled to Mexico on several occasions and also frequently stopped by Mexico City on the way to and from
Chile, where my own academic interests had taken me.

Víctor came to California to visit three or four times. He'd made quite a
lot of money selling desalination devices to Pemex, the Mexican state petroleum consortium, for their drilling platforms in the Gulf. He usually stayed
at the Mark Hopkins in San Francisco and drove up to the house. Víctor
was nearly my age but looked a lot younger: trim, handsome, enormously
gregarious, smart, and full of the affectionate insults typical of Mexican
humor. He was also a gracious, sparkling flirt, loved to dance, particularly
the cha-cha-cha, which he'd learned when that music first arrived in Mexico
with the Orquesta América from Cuba in the mid-fifties.

In 1957 he'd met Fidel Castro's sister Enma in the Sanborns restaurant
under the American Embassy on the Reforma Avenue, and three years later
they were married in Havana. That was another reason to keep up with Víctor, because my interest in the Cuban Revolution is what got me started in
studying Latin America in the first place.

Víctor's wit and charm had earned him social and political capital that enabled him to thrive in the years of the "Mexican Miracle." By the early nineties, he had made enough to buy a delightful summer place in the subtropics just south of Cuernavaca and to acquire three cars and a number of expensive paintings for the house in Mexico City. On two occasions, Alex and I had gone down to visit Víctor and Enma's place in Chiconcuac.

During a visit to Víctor's tropical paradise—it must have been late September or early October 2005, or in any case after Gutiérrez Esquivel seemed more likely to be the Cardona's owner—we sat under umbrellas around the pool and drank a couple of tequilas, neat, with salt and lime. I remember that Enma (not Emma but "En-ma, as in *en mayo*," Víctor used to correct me) had a margarita. There was a lunch of *pozole* and simple *tacos de pollo* followed by a *siestecita*. After a nap, Víctor and Alex plunged into the pool and splashed around, maybe, I thought, a little too playfully.

Later in the afternoon, we walked a few blocks to the village of Chiconcuac, where the main attraction was the spectacular ruin of a great colonial sugar plantation. Alex and I walked in silence behind Víctor and Enma, Alex examining the bougainvillea hanging on the adobe walls.

The guidebooks like to describe the plantations (or haciendas) as "founded by the conquistador Hernán Cortés," but in fact most weren't. And their prosperous era was, in fact, the last half of the nineteenth century, when steam and rail led to profits and impressive new stone construction in the so-called colonial style. Hundreds of white-clad peasants had once lived in humble houses in the shadow of the sugar mill and, one imagined, filed quietly into the hacienda chapel for the sacraments. On the day we visited the hacienda, young Mexicans in jeans and sneakers idly hung out on the cast-iron benches around the rusted Porfirian bandstand with cans of Coke and Esquimo ice cream bars.

Hacienda Chiconcuac had once been a sprawling, thick-walled sugar plantation and now lay mostly in ruins. Rough plank scaffolding partly blocked the entrance to the hacienda, but an itinerant priest still performed Sunday morning mass in the hacienda chapel. Enma covered her reddish blonde hair with a lace handkerchief and entered while I sat on a stone bench in the courtyard. Víctor, who entered churches only for weddings and baptisms, and then only awkwardly, suggested that the three of us climb the crumbling walls of the hacienda to get a good look at the ruin. When I demurred, Víctor gave Alex his arm, lifting her lightly up to a row of huge limestone blocks, and they went cheerfully off.

Enma came out of the chapel after a bit, and we struck up a conversation.

Actually, it was the continuation of a conversation I usually have with her about her background in Cuba, her early years with the famous brother on the family *finca* in Oriente province, what Fidel was like as a teenager, and so on. "Obstreperous," she once told me, using the English word, "but who wouldn't have been with a father who hung up a dozen pictures of General Franco in the house?" Enma was one of seven siblings in the Castro Ruz family. Unlike Juanita, who broke with Fidel in the first years of the revolution, Enma remained in familial solidarity, but not uncritical solidarity, with her brother and his island. She had fallen in love with Víctor and made her life in Mexico City.

When Víctor and Alex returned from their climb, he explained to the three of us that Hernán Cortés himself had founded Chiconcuac, and it had been sacked and left to ruin by the Zapatistas after 1910. Later it was abandoned by the owner and then acquired, perhaps in the forties and fifties, by Tyrone Power. Power and his Mexican wife, Linda Christian—a legendary beauty and the subject of two portraits by Diego Rivera—were in Mexico making the movie *Captain from Castile* in those years.

I remembered that Robert Barlow, of all people, had helped out with the Nahuatl dialogue in *Captain from Castile*. I asked who owned the place now.

"An architect, a wealthy architect. That's the guy who's beginning to restore it, the chapel and all," said Víctor. "We met him here a year or two ago. I don't remember his name. Maybe González or Gómez something."

Enma turned to Víctor. "Oye, chico! Remember, he was involved with the reconstruction of the Franz Mayer, Gutiérrez Esquivel."

"Víctor never goes to museums," she explained with affectionate disapproval. "Gutiérrez is a *coleccionista*, and he's restoring the hacienda as a place for his *colecciones*."

"Don't you remember, Víctor?" she asked in Spanish. "We saw El Arquitecto here, I think at a baptism. *De todas maneras*, he's given this place a very pretentious name, 'El Palacio del Marqués.' Maybe he thinks he's the new Marqués!"

Enma turned and explained to Alex, "Hernán Cortés, who Víctor thinks built this hacienda, but I know didn't, was known as 'El Marqués del Valle.'"

Coincidence, they say, is rife in life, but trite and implausible in stories. Well, this was life. And a much greater coincidence than anything I could have invented. Could it really be that Guillermo Gutiérrez Esquivel, the man who had sent the unsigned letter praising the Cardona to the Getty, the man I'd been trying to find since that afternoon in the Crocker Lab twenty years ago, was the owner of both the codex and this hacienda? That he was restoring the old estate as a place for his *colecciones*, and I'd stumbled on it by sheer chance? Indeed, was it not possible that at this very moment, just a few yards away in one of the restored rooms of the Hacienda Chiconcuac, Gutiérrez Esquivel had the Codex Cardona under lock and key?

I certainly wasn't prepared to explain to Víctor and Enma the incredible confluence of events that might have put me and the codex together in this Mexican village. On an earlier visit, I had mentioned to Víctor that I was working on a kind of Mexican mystery, but he had showed only polite interest, so I dropped the story. Now I had to think of ways to find Gutiérrez Esquivel. Perhaps Enma, who has all kinds of connections in the Mexican art world, would intercede with El Arquitecto for me. I knew I'd need an introduction.

But I was getting far ahead of the story. I didn't know—in fact, I had no *real* reason for suspecting—that this distinguished architect was now or had ever been the owner of the Codex Cardona. His letter in the Getty file did indicate, however, that he at least knew of its existence, and Nicholas Olsberg, moreover, had remembered that the man who'd written that letter may have had something to do with the Cardona. Olsberg probably knew more than he was letting on. Also, Enma made Gutiérrez Esquivel sound like a high-end *coleccionista*, and he was certainly building a fancy place to store his collections. Then, too, it wasn't impossible that he was the partner—who had been described as an architect—of the man who had called Stephen Colston for an evaluation of the sixteenth-century document just before its appearance at Christie's in New York. But then again—the caveats and qualifications never ended—Chris Coover at Christie's had said that Gutiérrez Esquivel was "not the name we had."

But of course he wouldn't reveal his name, would he?

How to reach El Arquitecto? How to persuade him—no doubt a private, if not hidden, man—to talk with me? I'd found nothing on the Internet; there were no listings in the Mexico City telephone books; there was no office at the Hacienda Chiconcuac; only a few construction workers desultorily wheelbarrowing stones and overgrown vines and trees from the outer walls. Obviously lots of people in Mexico City knew Gutiérrez Esquivel, but I didn't know any of them. Strange how hard it was to find such a high-profile person and how very much harder it would be to actually get him to talk with me. Enma Castro might be a point of entry because of her association with people who likely moved in Gutiérrez Esquivel's circle.

We drove back to Mexico City in the weekend traffic over the south rim of the Valley of Mexico and down into the teeming city of twenty million. Alex, sitting beside me in the back seat of the Peugeot, was looking straight ahead, a little nervous about Víctor's driving. The city lights stretched as far as you could see, west, north, and east. I remembered the first time I'd seen this view; it must have been over forty years ago, coming back from water-skiing on Lake Tequesquitengo with Víctor and a couple of his university friends. I'd felt then like I was looking out on a strange new planet. Down there, some 450 years ago, in what then was the hemisphere's most extensive city, I could imagine Aztec painter-scribes, urged on by Spanish friars, trimming *amate* into folio-sized sheets, dipping their brushes into local pigments, and working away on a marvelous painted book. What had Captain Alonzo Cardona y Villaviciosa, the crown official responsible for the work, done with the codex that now bears his name? What route had it taken to end up, perhaps now hidden away, in don Guillermo Gutiérrez Esquivel's restored hacienda? There were many possible paths to follow; perhaps someone knew the right one. I still didn't.

In the morning, I waited for an hour to call Víctor because I knew they slept late.

"Bíctor," I said, pronouncing the V in the Mexican way, "I have to come out this morning to see both of you. Is that possible?" I gave a brief explanation and appealed to our many years of friendship.

He answered with mock, maybe real, irritation.

"Ay, qué te pasa?" he said. "Tanto apuro." *What's with you? Such a rush.* I heard him call for Enma.

"Bueno, we'll be here," he said. "Give us an hour."

I took the hotel taxi to Colonia Rosedal. Víctor came out to open a formidable steel door set into a tall cement wall and led me past three cars into the house to greet Enma. A large oil painting I remembered from my last visit seemed much larger, covering almost an entire wall in the living room. A portrait of Enma hung over the piano. I was struck again by how tranquil Mexican houses can be in the midst of all the street noise.

"That was really nice being in Chiconcuac yesterday," I began, and then, turning to Enma, made my pitch. The words came out of me in a rush:

"Look, I know Víctor thinks I'm a bit batty about this story and that I've been talking about it for a long time, but now I think I've found the owner of the codex and perhaps it's Gutiérrez Esquivel, El Arquitecto, the man of the Hacienda Chiconcuac. I have to talk with him to finish the story. I won't give you all the details, but it's very important for me. Víctor and I have been friends for over forty years, imagine! And now I really need your help."

I went on a bit like this and then mentioned that since Enma said she had spoken with El Arquitecto about some Cuban paintings on the day of the baptism, I wondered if she would feel comfortable inquiring whether he would meet with me. I told her that I had tried a few months earlier with no success, and acknowledged that he might not in fact want to see me. But would she ask?

Enma left, came back with a leather-bound address book, flipped through the pages, thought, leafed some more.

"Oye, I don't think I can help much with Gutiérrez. And really, I can't remember exactly what he wanted. I do know that he's also a big figure here, very busy, a big shot in the Centro Histórico project. It would be hard; men like that don't give you much of their time. But maybe — Víctor, what do you think? Maybe Fofo and Orquidia?"

Enma explained that they had contributed to the Franz Mayer reconstruction and knew Gutiérrez then. They also, I remembered, had helped Fidel acquire the boat *Granma* for the 1956 landing in Oriente Province.

"How long are you here, I mean in Mexico?" she asked.

I could sense interminable chasing around, and in the end, nothing.

"Just one more day; Alex is going back this morning."

Enma went into another room to call. I couldn't make out the words, but judging from the tone of the long conversation, it didn't sound hopeful. When she came back, she shook her head.

"It's been quite a while since they were involved with the Franz Mayer. Orquidia didn't feel right about ringing up Gutiérrez. Let me think some more. Maybe someone can help; I can see it's important to you."

We finished the thin coffee the *empleada* brought, and Víctor walked me out. On the street, waiting for the radio taxi, another connection occurred to me.

"Víctor, remember in the fifties, you were friends with Antonio Capilla, the Olympic diver, and his brother — what was his name? I knew him too?"

"Beto. He was going with Cristina then. Remember?"

"Yes, I do. So did you ever meet another Olympic champion in those years, Tonatiuh Gutiérrez?"

"Of course."

How could he not have? Víctor knew everyone. There was a small world within this city of twenty million souls.

"I knew him well," Víctor said. "He died three or four years ago. We flew together to an economic conference in Hamburg back when I was in the Ministry, and then we saw each other several times afterward here and there."

"What about his wife, his widow, Electra López Mompradé?"

"I never met her. She lives here in Coyoacán, in Belisario Domínguez Street; I don't know the street number."

"Víctor," I said, firing my last shot, "I think that Tonatiuh and Gutiérrez Esquivel were good friends. Do you think that you could get in touch with Electra and ask for El Arquitecto's current phone number? That's all, just the phone number?"

I couldn't go through all the background, or the background that I'd imagined, of Tonatiuh and Gutiérrez Esquivel while standing in the street waiting for the taxi. Víctor, I thought, could explain that I had only a personal, academic interest in colonial artifacts and the Centro Histórico, that I was not a buyer, and that I wasn't interested in any old legal flaps.

I went back to the María Cristina, had some hot cakes with cool coffee and lay down for a nap, wiped out; the seven-thousand-foot elevation didn't help. This was no country for old men, I was beginning to think.

Around five that afternoon, Víctor called the numbers he had for Electra. Two were disconnected, but a third answered.

"La señora Electra no longer lives at this number," a woman told Víctor; nor, she continued, did she know Electra's current address. "She no longer lives in Mexico."

CHAPTER TWELVE

Librería Zócalo

In Mexico, we can falsify *anything*.

JAIME ORTÍZ JAFOUS

 During the Christmas break in 2005, my young colleague Andrés Reséndez rang up. He had just returned from a conference in Mexico City. It was a rushed two-day trip, but since the conference met in the renovated Centro Histórico district, he found time between sessions to look up a friend, a well-known rare book dealer called don Ignacio Bernal. As a graduate student, Andrés had spent a few years in Mexico doing research for Televisa's history-based soap operas and had gotten to know the Librería Zócalo and Ignacio Bernal quite well.

"We went around the corner for coffee," Andrés told me; "Don Ignacio carries out most of his business there, always at the same place." They went over the local book gossip, talked about chronicles and documents relating to the Cabeza de Vaca adventure—Andrés's current research project. When Andrés brought up the subject of the Codex Cardona (as I had asked him to), Bernal became quite animated; in fact, Andrés missed one of the conference sessions because he got so caught up in talking about the Cardona. A few years ago, Bernal told Andrés, the codex had been a *secreto a voces*, open gossip. It had apparently been offered to an important and very wealthy banker, and the word got around to a handful of people.

Bernal was one of three people asked to evaluate the Cardona in the banker's office. "Very mysterious, the whole thing," he told Andrés. Two scholars, one local, one French, had dismissed the codex out of hand, in part, Bernal thought, because of the paper, but also because *they* had not previously heard of it. Bernal thought their offhand dismissal was less than professional. "He's inclined to believe the codex could be a *falsificación*," Andrés told me, but Bernal also thought that the academic specialists, who had really only looked at the paper, were too cavalier in their attitude.

We were sitting in my university office, and Andrés was telling me about his meeting with don Ignacio. "He'd be willing to have a good long talk with you," Andrés said. "As you can imagine, he deals with lots of foreigners, especially academics from the U.S. and Europe, since he has one of the most important stores of old books in Mexico. He also keeps his own counsel; but I think you two would hit it off quite well, and he could be helpful. Some gringo academics can be quite know-it-all—*prepotente* is the word he likes to use—but if he sees you're serious and know as much as you do about the Codex Cardona, he might open up. You could talk about Mexico in the fifties and sixties; the two of you must be about the same age."

Andrés warmed to the subject. He was excited by the new leads I'd uncovered; the script was heating up. Don Ignacio Bernal would show me around, Andrés said, and might introduce me to Electra López Momprodé. "He knows her and knew Tonatiuh, who, by the way, was also an important collector. He even mentioned a man—he referred to him as an 'anonymous dealer'—who claimed that he had been involved with two attempts to sell the codex, first at Sotheby's and then in the United States." Bernal didn't know where, and he wasn't forthcoming with the anonymous dealer's name; Andrés felt that he shouldn't push. Andrés didn't know if Bernal knew Gutiérrez Esquivel personally, but he would certainly know people who did, and maybe a connection could be made. "I remember," Andrés said wistfully, "that you and I weren't very successful with our phone call."

Andrés remembered something else. "There may be more to this 'anonymous dealer.' I think don Ignacio and *el anónimo* worked together on some sales; in any case, they have some sort of relationship. If you went to Mexico, perhaps you could find the 'anonymous dealer' and other players. You *can't* do this by phone or e-mail; you have to go talk to don Ignacio face to face and see where that leads. I'm telling you, I had a really good talk with him. As it is, you're in a sort of good news–bad news place. The good news is that you have new leads and characters; the bad news is that the codex has disappeared. I'd guess, after talking to don Ignacio, that it's vanished into an invisible, private realm."

I must have emitted a deep sigh. In our five years together at the university, I'd not seen Andrés so steamed up, so enthusiastic. With so much new information crowding in, I didn't know for the moment where to take the conversation, so I asked about the conference, how his presentation had gone, about the people there whom we both knew.

But Andrés returned to the codex. "Speaking of disappearing," he said, "whatever happened to all those slides that the guy at the Getty used for an evaluation? They must be around."

I told him that Wim de Wit at the Getty had said they'd been returned to the agent, and Schwarz had told me he sent them to Tonatiuh, in Mexico. Tonatiuh was dead, so the slides were likely lost. Maybe Electra had them? But she was in Spain. I was throwing up obstacles; it all suddenly seemed very difficult.

"Look," Andrés said, raising his hands, palms toward me, "even if you haven't yet been able to get in touch personally with Gutiérrez Esquivel, you should get on the ground in Mexico City, poke around, talk to everyone you can. El Arquitecto is well known; there has to be a way to reach him. At a minimum you should also find the 'anonymous dealer.' By the way, don Ignacio doesn't do e-mail."

Should, should. I *should* do all these things. I didn't really feel at that moment like dragging my tired body around Mexico City, especially because it was so hard to walk, and in that city there's always lots of walking. I'd really have to be tuned in to get all the details, the nuances, the implications, and the impatient repetitions in any conversations I might be able to arrange. But it was true: the person I really *had* to see was El Arquitecto; maybe Ignacio Bernal *would* be the entry there. There were times, and this was one of them, when it all seemed too much. Maybe I could find someone to come with me, even *pay* someone to go along. And money was another worry; Mexico is no longer inexpensive.

That night, after listening to Andrés, I remembered that I'd heard from graduate students who had gone to Mexico about a "really great book dealer" on Calle Madero; but they'd never mentioned his name, maybe didn't know it. In any case, the book dealer had been helpful, and the students were impressed. A visit to don Ignacio Bernal was worth a shot.

After New Year's Day 2006—I was on sabbatical leave—I flew to Mexico City, took an official cab from the airport, and checked into the María Cristina on Río Lerma Street. The next morning I arranged for the hotel taxi to take me down the Avenida de la Reforma, then to Juárez past the Palace of Fine Arts—which everyone used to condemn as the ugliest building in the entire republic—and on to Calle Madero. It was a good idea to take an official taxi and not one off the street, because unlike taxis in some countries where passengers attack the driver, in Mexico in these days the *taxistas* assault the passengers.

The Librería Zócalo is right in the heart of the old colonial core, five or six blocks from the Sanborns Casa de Azulejos (House of Tile), a historic restaurant known to every tourist who has gone to Mexico since 1910.

I was early, in time to stop at Sanborns for a self-indulgent breakfast of *chilaquiles* and *frijoles de la olla*, for which the restaurant is justly famed, along with disappointingly cold tortillas—a major sin in Mexico—and the inevitably insipid coffee. Being able to sit in the glorious seventeenth-century covered patio, however, and to remember other times here was consolation enough.

As I ate, I remembered books with the old Casasola photographs of the revolution showing a heavy-lidded, scar-faced *campesino* sitting with four other Zapatistas with cartridge belts slung over their shoulders, all jostling for the cameraman's attention. In 1911 they had been sitting at the Sanborns counter, just around the corner from my table. The sleek young Mexican men having breakfast around me now, most of them talking on cell phones, were the products of the Revolution. But the big money, the cash to buy fancy cars, paintings, and even sixteenth-century codices, was in Coyoacán, or up in Las Lomas and beyond, in the palatial homes of the new rich. Ironic, I thought, that some of these people, beneficiaries of a nationalist and indigenous revolution, were now engaged in selling abroad the priceless objects of their national patrimony.

No doubt I should have called the bookstore for an appointment—or had someone call for me—and now I didn't want to barge in on don Ignacio Bernal; everyone described him as a kind of Old World gentleman and scholar. Nor did I want to get off on the wrong foot by brusquely introducing the codex right off, though I knew Andrés had spoken to Bernal about me. I also knew, more so than Andrés, that all sorts of uncertainties and shady dealings surrounded the Cardona, so that discretion was in order.

I walked past the bookstore, a little apprehensive about going in; besides, I wanted to scout out some titles in the window displays. After all, I was a scholar, too; but I wasn't a specialist on the early colonial period, and I knew that Bernal was.

Easing up to the counter, a proprietor-like figure nowhere in sight, I fool-ishly came up with the idea of asking one of the clerks if she had a certain book by a Frenchman about the history of water and society in the Valley of Mexico. I was prepared to buy it, an indication of my good faith and also as something to take back to my friend David, since the history of water and society was his latest research project. The book wasn't available, but the clerk took me back into the bowels of the shop to show me a whole shelf of arcane works on water issues. I leafed through a half dozen but didn't select any to buy; they were all very expensive.

When I came out from the shelves, I casually asked if don Ignacio Bernal were available. I was told that he had gone out for coffee but would return "ahorrita," that is, "right away," an unpredictable length of time. Waiting for him to return, I browsed among the shelves, running my fingers over the spines of books I'd heard of and read about but never actually seen.

Bernal didn't appear, so I strolled down to the far end of Madero Street where it opened onto the huge plaza known by all Mexicans today as the Zócalo, for which, of course, the bookstore was named. Here I was stand-ing just a few yards from the former site of the Aztec Templo Mayor and the palace of Moctezuma himself. Five hundred years ago, in the artisanal quarters surrounding this central plaza, craftsmen would have been work-ing precious metals and exotic feathers into exquisite adornments. Just to the north, had I been able to return to that time, I'd have found a great many *tlahcuiloyan*, "the place where one writes and paints." There, near what is today the Plaza Santo Domingo, the streets might have been alive with dozens of painters and scribes making painted books long before the Spaniards arrived in November 1519. After the conquest, the *tlahcuilos* had continued their tradition under the direction of Franciscan and Domini-can friars. Maybe there the folios of the Codex Mendoza or the Telleriano-Remensis, maybe even the Codex Cardona and the great maps that accom-panied it, were put together 450 years ago.

Later, in the arcades near the Plaza Santo Domingo, colonial scribes charged a few *reales* to write letters of longing for their lovelorn but illiter-ate fellow citizens. That honorable tradition, in the same place but on raised platforms under awnings, was continued with Underwood typewriters dur-ing my student days in Mexico. I used to watch the humble men, young and old, stand twisting their hats, hoping that their sentiments would be adequately expressed. Today that service still goes on, now with laptops and portable printers.

I returned to the Librería Zócalo and browsed again until Bernal returned. I introduced myself, mentioning "el joven" Andrés Reséndez, explaining that I was a history professor at the University of California and remarking on the shop's impressive collection of ancient works on water. This was an awkward, roundabout introduction to the conversation I wanted to have, and it must surely have puzzled don Ignacio; but he acknowledged with a nod that Reséndez had mentioned me.

Ignacio Bernal was a cultivated, affable man of perhaps sixty with a trim gray beard and a wry, worldly manner. He also came across as a warm, gentle man. No doubt he had much experience with foreign clients, though he appeared not to speak English. I plunged right into my story, telling him how nearly fifteen years ago I had come across the codex known as the Cardona when it was being offered for sale to an American university. I told him that though I was not a specialist in ancient manuscripts, I'd been poking around ever since seeing the Cardona, to try to solve some of the mystery about it and maybe even write some sort of a story.

I explained that I'd had the opportunity to talk with at least a half-dozen specialists on the subject of the Cardona, who had actually held the codex in their hands, studied it carefully, and written evaluations. Of the evaluators, three or four thought it authentic; a couple had doubts. Moreover, none of the people at the places it had been offered — and rejected — knew whether it had ever been sold or where it might be today. Then, to show I was into the subject, I mentioned Tonatiuh Gutiérrez. "Perhaps you know his widow, Electra López Mompradé?"

Bernal looked at me, vaguely acknowledging my question. "What else?" he seemed to be asking.

"Several of your clients, including young Reséndez," I continued, still very stiffly, "told me that you have your finger on the pulse of the rare book and manuscript trade and that if I came to Mexico, it would be worth looking you up. So here I am. In fact, I'd be happy with whatever scraps of information you could give me about the Codex Cardona."

Bernal ignored the remark about Tonatiuh. "I'm not sure it's a very vital pulse," he said. "Selling old books is a pretty sclerotic trade. I'd be pleased to talk with you about the Codex Cardona. I don't know a lot; but as you can see, I happen to have several clients around this morning. It's not common. If you can come back in, say, half an hour?"

After he finished with his clients, Bernal told me that he had no idea where the Cardona is today. He had a few names to suggest, though, if

I wanted to try to track down its story and what had become of it. With regard to Tonatiuh, he said that he had been a friend and that he'd died a few years back. It would be easy to get in touch with his widow, Electra López Momprodé, who Bernal thought lived out in Coyoacán. He thought that Tonatiuh might indeed have had something to do with the Cardona, and Electra would no doubt know something; the trick was getting to see her.

I didn't say so, but of course my efforts on that front had already led to naught, and Bernal's information regarding Electra was out of date. Though I was exhausted from my flight and short of breath because of the altitude, I felt I was finally making progress. Don Ignacio Bernal and I were hitting it off pretty well. When we sat down in the back of the store, his voice took on a more confidential tone.

The recent news, he told me, leaning forward, was that the owner of the codex had kept out of sight; no one knew for sure who he was. Bernal didn't know the full story; maybe, he said, no one did. There was still a lot of gossip floating about. But rumor had it that the owner was—or had been—Guillermo Gutiérrez Esquivel. Gutiérrez was a well-known architect and *coleccionista*, Bernal continued, and a big dog in the project to restore the old colonial Hospital de Betlemitas that had received substantial donations from Mexican banks and, he thought, from men like Carlos Slim, the Teléfonos de Mexico billionaire—the wealthiest man in Latin America.

Gutiérrez Esquivel himself, Bernal said, lived in a fancy house up in Lomas de Chapultepec; owned—or had owned—a house in Puerto Vallarta, and owned an old ruined plantation in the state of Morelos, the Hacienda Chiconcuac, which he was restoring on his own. He also had something to do with the Museo Franz Mayer. "A real jewel, as I'm sure you know." Bernal also imagined that Gutiérrez Esquivel might have appropriated more than a few colonial artifacts—old ledger books, documents, other things—that his teams of excavators had found hidden away in convents and the conquistadors' early mansions. Some of these, he believed, had ended up in the Franz Mayer, and others might have been sold to antiquarians in Mexico and elsewhere.

But then—Bernal wasn't sure just when or how this happened—Gutiérrez Esquivel apparently got himself into hot water with an overrun of millions of dollars as part of the Centro Histórico project. Or maybe he ran off with the funds or failed to deliver. In any case, the Banco de México sued him, and as Bernal recalled, he was even jailed for a time. Bernal had the impression, but wasn't certain, that the bank took the big house in Lomas and maybe even the Hacienda Chiconcuac.

"People say that Gutiérrez Esquivel has now changed his name," Bernal concluded, "and has disappeared from the scene." As for the Cardona, there was also some talk that a well-known dealer in antiquities here in Mexico City named Rodrigo Rivero Lake was somehow involved. "But I can't get into that particular tangled tale right now"—*enmarañado cuento*, Bernal called it—"I've only heard rumors."

The flood of new information astounded me. Bernal's name had been mentioned by my graduate students but I had not followed up—after all, there are many rare book dealers in Mexico City—concentrating instead on Schwarz, the curators at the Getty and Christie's, and the academic specialists who had vetted the codex. But then, too, none of this new, and perhaps not wholly accurate, information would have come to light had it not been for the recent scandal surrounding Gutiérrez Esquivel. Until now, the Cardona had moved silently, underground, among private owners and circumspect and perhaps dishonest dealers, who were understandably guarded given the doubts about provenance and about the legality of the codex's sale abroad.

It occurred to me that Bernal, clearly fascinated by the strange saga of the Cardona, might have been inclined to embellish the story. I had seen the Hacienda Chiconcuac only a few months earlier, and people seemed to think it still belonged to "El señor Arquitecto"; I wondered if he had really changed his name.

The next evening, I was surprised by a message at the hotel from Bernal, asking if we could have a midmorning coffee at his store. He had some news for me. Eleven o'clock would be good.

Don Ignacio was waiting for me with a friendly greeting, and this time we went down the street to his favorite espresso place. He nodded hello to a handful of regular clients as we sat at a small, marble-topped table under a tin Coca-Cola umbrella.

"I've thought some more about your codex and talked to a couple of people last night," he said. "It passed through a number of hands a few years ago, and most people here thought it was a *falsificación*, mainly because of the paper."

I acknowledged that the same objections had been made in London and California.

"It wasn't just that such an important, official document should have been on European paper at that time, three decades after the conquest," Bernal said. "It's that the *amate* was the wrong color. Almost all legitimate sixteenth-century *amate* documents I've seen are darker, a dark tan or brown. The codex we're talking about was lighter, more like present-day *amate*. I can tell you that I saw the Codex Cardona in the office of an important official in Banamex—the Bank of Mexico. The man in charge of the banker's *colecciones*, which are impressive, asked me, along with two specialists, or self-declared specialists, for an opinion on the codex's authenticity."

I'd heard this from Andrés but didn't interrupt.

"My conclusion was 'puede que si, puede que no,' that the codex could be authentic and also may not be. You probably know that *amate* is made today."

"I did know that," I said. "When, more or less, did this happen, when you saw the codex?"

"Maybe some seven, eight, years ago." That would have been 1998–99.

We sipped our coffee, and Bernal took out his cell phone and called his store. In a few minutes a woman appeared with two splendid facsimiles of well-known *libros de pintura*, one of them a fragment of the "Matrícula de tributos," a section of the Codex Mendoza. Both the paper and the paint looked suitably old to my untrained eye, and the paleography looked absolutely to be authentic sixteenth-century script. But these documents were actually present-day copies; the frontispiece was dated 2005.

"A *tlahcuilo* I know made these over the past several months. They go for about $2,500 dollars apiece. This is far from really professional-grade work; they're made for the tourist trade. But even then you can see that the ancient art hasn't been lost."

As we talked, a rotund older man, jolly, with a full beard and thick glasses, strolled up to our table, greeting Bernal as if he hadn't seen him in some time. The two talked, rather haltingly, as if Bernal wanted the man to go away. But he continued to stand there; and with some misgivings, I asked him if he'd care to join us, hoping that he wouldn't, because I wanted the time alone with Bernal. The man sat down, however, and Bernal added another espresso to his tab. The man was an architect called Jaime Ortíz Jafous, an unusual name I didn't get the first couple of times Bernal repeated it.

"Jaime knows Gutiérrez Esquivel," Bernal said, "and worked with him on the Franz Meyer." Turning to Ortíz, he said, "Our friend here is interested in a curious sixteenth-century codex that Gutiérrez has, or at least had."

Ortíz knew Gutiérrez Esquivel fairly well; not only had he worked with him on the museum project, but he had visited Chiconcuac several times to see his collections. Ortíz's dropping by was yet another of the fortuitous coincidences that accompanied my search for the Cardona. I thought that because of his long association, Ortíz might give me some insight into Gutiérrez Esquivel, but he didn't offer much. He knew about his work on the Hospital de Betlemitas — "Just there," he said, pointing up Gante Street, "on Cinco de Mayo. Go look. It's beautifully restored. Banamex has now taken it over." I got the impression that along with his admiration, Ortíz found Gutiérrez flamboyant, extravagant, and rather intolerant of tastes other than his own.

The talk then turned to the Codex Cardona, which Ortíz had vaguely heard of but never seen. Ortíz was leafing through the codex facsimiles that Bernal had placed on the table, commenting on the excellent work of present-day *tlahcuilos*, when I said to Bernal:

"Now tell me seriously. You think the Cardona is a *falsificación*, but we're talking 427 pages, three hundred illustrations, a couple of spectacular maps. Would it *really* be possible for someone, even a team of forgers, to work up something like the Cardona? Who could have done it? It's one thing to *copy* a known codex" — I indicated the facsimiles — "but something else to do it from scratch. The Cardona is a work of great erudition; it would have to be someone like León-Portilla. Or a Robert Barlow," I added with a laugh.

"Given that choice, I'd put my money on Barlow," Bernal said with a smile.

"*Mira*," Ortíz said, "here in Mexico we can falsify *anything*."

Ortíz bid us good day and ambled up Gante, but Bernal was in no hurry to return to his store. He raised two fingers to the woman at the espresso machine, and over more coffee we continued to talk about Gutiérrez Esquivel, the reconstruction of the Centro Histórico, and possible buyers of the codex. Later, walking back to the store, he turned to a different subject, one he seemed to have kept in reserve.

"Yesterday, when you were in my store," he said, "just a half hour after you left, a business acquaintance I hadn't seen for several months walked in. He's another rare book and antiquities dealer, a successful one. Over the years, he and I saw each other now and then, and I got to know him a bit. Too well, in fact; he owes me money! I remembered that he'd had something to do with the Cardona, so I mentioned your visit (not your name!). In the course of our conversation, he offhandedly mentioned that, yes, he'd been involved with the codex at Sotheby's in London in the early eighties (he hadn't been sure who the owner was then) and again, six or seven years ago, in New York."

Bernal didn't offer his friend's name; and when I wondered aloud about the man's identity, he wasn't forthcoming, so I didn't push it. There was a pause, however, and I asked if this was the man that Bernal had referred to as the "anonymous dealer" when he talked to Andrés.

"Actually, I don't see why I should be so guarded about his real name— he's had more than one. The man's name, not his original name, is Franz Friedmann Fierro. He's Mexican-Jewish, some say a former member of the Israeli Mossad. And others might tell you that he's one of Rivero Lake's accomplices."

"He's an exotic figure," Bernal continued, "goes around Mexico in a huge, armored *todo terreno* SUV with bullet-proof glass—well, lots of people do that these days—knows all the important clients for books and objets d'art, knows the Cardona, knows Gutiérrez, knows the high-end dealer Rodrigo Rivero Lake—all the main players in your story. I think he's worked with Rivero Lake on a number of sales and consignments."

Bernal went on to tell me a "little story" about Franz Friedmann.

"Friedmann came in one day, and we were standing in the store talking with maybe three or four clients. Suddenly there was a sharp click behind him, like a dry twig breaking—maybe someone had snapped his glasses case shut. Friedmann wheeled in a flash, looking for the weapon, front claws raised like a panther ready to spring. It was *impresionante*. He's not your ordinary dealer of old books, and not the kind of man you'd want to mess with."

I didn't like the sound of that. Recalling that Schwarz had once thought Tonatiuh "menacing," I thought of the stories about the abusive plain-clothes Judicial Police and the thugs they hired to resolve delicate cases. Lots of money, millions in the case of the Cardona, could, I imagined, lead to informal ways of suppressing unwanted publicity.

I returned quickly to the codex. "Did you ever learn anything more about the business in New York? I mean where the codex went or whom it was sold to after it was offered at Christie's and rejected?"

"Well, this is my surprise for you," Bernal said. "I asked Friedmann that question just now, this last time he was in the store. He told me directly, right to my face, that he had sold the Codex Cardona in Barcelona to a big-time *hotelero*, the owner of a hotel chain. That's all I know, and you can take it for what it's worth. I doubt that Friedmann knows where the codex is now; moreover, the story itself may not be true."

All fascinating, of course. Finally it seemed that several strands of my research were coming together, even if I still had only loose ends in hand. Bernal saw me wondering what to do next. "I have Friedmann's telephone number here in Mexico, which I'll give you, but I doubt very much that he'll agree to meet with you or even talk with you. And if I were you"—Bernal touched his forefinger just below his right eye as if to say, be careful there!— "I'd think twice about dealing with Friedmann."

It's not, I gathered, that these people will break your kneecaps, but they have ways to intimidate, to discourage awkward questions. There was a lot at stake in the Cardona transaction, the questions of origin, fraud, authenticity, and illegal sale, for starters. And money: that's what heats everything up. We talked for a few minutes more, but the subject of Friedmann and the Codex Cardona had dried up.

I said a fond farewell to don Ignacio and slowly walked west down Madero Street, past the Iturbide Palace on my left. I stopped at the entrance to the Franciscan church. This was one of the eighty Franciscan churches and convents that the order founded in Mexico during the first thirty years after the conquest, and the original part of the building here was the oldest, dating back to the early 1520s. Pedro de Gante—Peter of Ghent, a "nephew," probably an informal son, of Charles V—was one of the first members of the congregation.

In those early decades after the arrival of the invading Spaniards, along with the reconstruction of the fallen Aztec capital and the single-minded devotion to evangelizing the native people, the core of the old city must have been abuzz with the discovery of intimidating stone idols, the burning of some libros de pintura and the making of others. Every day, new remnants of the vanquished culture must have surfaced among the ruins while the Franciscans and Dominicans leaned over the native Aztec scribes working to preserve for the Europeans a record of their own past life. In fact, in this very church, some of the Franciscan friars had preserved a copy of the tonalámatl, the Aztecs' 260-day almanac that Bernardino de Sahagún, later the author of the Florentine Codex, wished to destroy.[1]

The Codex Cardona itself may not have been compiled here (maybe parts of it were), but the friars must have seen others like it, drawn up by Nahuatl-speaking painters and scribes some 450 years ago, maybe just blocks from here in this fascinating, maddening city. Well, I thought, thinking of don Ignacio's facsimiles, they're still at it.

Madero Street, once a place of stately homes, some turned into impressive banks, has become a bit tacky today, with its open-air gyro and hamburger stands and cheap jewelry stores. In 1840, when Fanny Calderón de la Barca, a Scotswoman who married a Spanish diplomat, rode down this street, she declared it "the handsomest street in Mexico." Looking up from her carriage in the early years of the Mexican republic, she remarked on a leftover member of the old Spanish aristocracy, the Marquesa de Aguayo, "who could be seen every day standing, smiling in her balcony, fat and fair."[2]

I came out of Madero alongside Bellas Artes, past the buckled pavement and all the swarming taxis. A flood of memories washed over me as I stood at the intersection remembering, a half century before, when I'd first come to Mexico City. The sights and smells, the new language, my Mexican friends, this incomprehensible country. Mexico was still a foreign country then, very different from anyplace else, though it turned out that the Mexicans who ran the place were soon straining to be like everyone else. That first winter, Víctor had invited me to the University of Mexico's formal ball, held just behind where I now stood, in the old Minería Building, described two hundred years earlier by Alexander von Humboldt. The ball represented Víctor's friends' acceptance of me and the beginning of a lifelong, if not untroubled, affair with this part of the world.

That was the first year, and thereafter whenever I left Mexico I always knew I'd return. And I had, maybe twenty, twenty-five, times. When you're young, you always know you'll be back; when you're old, it suddenly dawns on you that this may be the last time. I walked the long walk back to the hotel, and the next day, reluctant to look up señor Friedmann, I returned to California the second week of January, full of anticipation that I was really on the track of the codex and of its owner, whoever that might be.

CHAPTER THIRTEEN

An Internet Posting

His employees handed over the Codex Cardona to Rodrigo and
Francisco Rivero Lake, who were parked in their car outside no. 395
calle Barrilaco, in the upper-class district of Lomas de Chapultepec.

 Back from Mexico in early January 2006, I settled into my
home office, alternating between the pruning of my half-
acre vineyard (Syrah and Tempranillo grapes) and working
up the notes taken during my talks with Ignacio Bernal. His
kindness was appreciated and the trove of new information useful and en-
couraging. I'd also become better friends with Google, trolling the Internet
for every name and subject that could imaginably be related to the Codex
Cardona, but I hadn't had a good catch since my luck with the Blanco
Whites. Now, with don Ignacio's revelations, I had new names and sites
to investigate.

Rodrigo Rivero Lake, the "high-end antiquities dealer" whom Bernal had
mentioned, was all over the Internet: here pictured with his elegant wife,
there dining with the new—and a few of the old—moneyed elite in Mexico
City, or discussing his recent expensive, slick-paper books on antiquities.
The most recent work dealt with the Namban, or "southern barbarian" (i.e.,
the Portuguese), influence on sixteenth-century Japanese art and the subsequent transfer of elegant lecterns and paneled screens, or *byobu* (hispanized
as *biombo*), to the New World.

There were also charges against Rivero Lake for alleged shady dealings in
Peruvian antiquities. Tracking these leads led me eventually to the website
of Michel van Rijn, a Dutchman, variously described by his antagonists as a
smuggler, a charlatan, a police informer, and then—undergoing an appar-

ent change of skin—a philanthropic sleuth dedicated to exposing the rich field of fraud and illegal trafficking in the art and antiquities world. Highly controversial, his site was removed from Google in October 2006.

In Latin America, Van Rijn's major exposé dealt with the alleged theft of a series of oil paintings (other accounts called them frescos) from the ceiling of an eighteenth-century private chapel in a hacienda near the Inca capital of Cuzco in highland Peru. The entire ceiling of the chapel had been carefully dismantled, the panels shipped out from Peru for reassembly in Mexico. All of this had presumably taken place under the eyes of cooperative customs officials, and, of course, in flagrant violation of laws governing national patrimony.

Another allegation involving Rivero Lake had to do with the theft of a baroque altar, or *retablo*, from a church in Challapampa, also in Cuzco province. Rivero Lake won a favorable judgment in an apparently pliant Peruvian court; he nevertheless remained under considerable pressure from the Peruvian Ministry of Culture to return the altar to Cuzco.[1]

The culprit behind this caper, according to Van Rijn's lurid revelations, was Rodrigo Rivero Lake, a man Van Rijn called "Lake the Snake." But rather than stealing the paintings, Rivero Lake claimed he had actually *saved* them from the Shining Path, the guerrilla movement that ravaged Peru in the 1980s. Van Rijn nevertheless mounted on his website a dogged attack designed to expose Rivero Lake's pillaging of the pictures and the altar.

I clicked on the Van Rijn site often during the first months of 2006, looking for new postings, browsing his main site in the Spanish language preference, when an innocent-looking, incomplete, lower-case single entry entitled "un códice es mucho más . . ." barely caught my eye. In fact, it had been posted on January 1, 2006, but I had missed it. Curious, I scrolled down to a twelve-page document posted by a person self-identified as "the owner" or the "proprietor" of the Codex Cardona and also as the "sole administrator of the Palacio del Marqués," who claimed that Rivero Lake had *stolen* the codex from him. Van Rijn was now taking up the case of the "sole administrator of the Palacio del Marqués," turning his website's guns on "Lake the Snake" and the *codice* mentioned in the posting. Although the web posting didn't say so, the sole administrator of the Palacio del Marqués was, of course (or had to be, or certainly seemed to be), none other than Guillermo Gutiérrez Esquivel, the very same or *el mismísimo*, as the Mexicans would say—the heretofore anonymous figure who now, for the first time, seemed to reveal himself as the owner of the codex during its previous appearances at Sotheby's, the Getty, and Stanford. An incredible turn of events; I jumped back from my computer in surprise.

On the Van Rijn website, "the owner," writing in the first-person singular, produced an explanation—well, a *partial* explanation—of his involvement with the Cardona. In Spanish, he first set out the background—"los hechos," or "the facts"—of his current predicament. He began by presenting a judicial document showing that on June 27, 1994, he had established a corporation of which he was the sole administrator, "duly constituted in conformity with Mexican legislation," called El Palacio del Marqués, with an initial capital of US$15 million. This amount was made up of works of art enumerated in a document recognized as annex 1. The annex does not appear on the website, but the owner states that a principal piece in the collection was the document known as the *Relación Cardona*. This work, he claimed, had been evaluated "by experts" as worth $3.5 million, without taking into account the four-elephant-folio map of Mexico-Tenochtitlán and another map of equal size of Coyoacán, each valued at $1.3 million. The owner based this monetary evaluation of the codex solely on an offhand statement by Thomas Schwarz in a note included in the web page and addressed to no particular person. The note dates back to the Stanford negotiations in 1986.

The owner goes on to emphasize that the Cardona is "a colonial document of national interest, susceptible to being confiscated [*susceptible de apropiación*]," and can be sold only in Mexico, to a Mexican. This is a most curious remark, since another letter included in the posting, from James Fox of Stanford University, dated 1986, deals precisely with the owner's negotiations for the Cardona's sale in the United States at Stanford. And, of course, similar negotiations took place with Sotheby's and at the Getty, when the present owner was then presumably the owner of the codex. Actually, the owner is careful throughout the posting not to say outright that he *was* the codex's owner during these attempted sales; rather, he implies that the dealings with the Getty and Stanford were simply efforts to draw on "expert advice" to establish the document's authenticity. But the Fox letter says nothing about "authenticating"—only that Stanford is considering the *purchase* of the codex.

Nor does the owner make any reference to provenance—that is, where he obtained the Cardona. He does include a statement from Schwarz, similar to the notarized affidavit in the Stanford file that mentioned the eighteenth-century Spaniard Felipe Neve as a former owner of the "Mexican painted book." Someone, however, added a couple of centuries for good measure: the eighteenth-century ancestor now became, in the Internet posting, "a Spanish nobleman, an important functionary in the *sixteenth* century." Schwarz's statement reiterates the notarized affidavit's information, that the codex was purchased in 1928 by Baron von Schultzenberg-León and sold again around 1950 to the "present owner." It's not clear who the "present owner" had come to be by 1950; but the affidavit, as we have seen, intended to establish that the Cardona is a document with long antecedents in Europe, not Mexico.

Does the Internet posting imply that the "present owner" actually *did* acquire the Cardona at that time, "around 1950," directly from Baron von Schultzenberg-León? Or from someone else in Britain? Or not there at all? If the present owner did indeed buy the Cardona from the baron around 1950, and, moreover, buy it in England, why didn't he allay the doubts raised by Sotheby's, the Getty, and Stanford by demonstrating that the Cardona had ancient Spanish antecedents, long removed from Mexico, and was thus arguably exempt from national patrimony laws? Instead Tonatiuh Gutiérrez produced, only under duress, the ambiguously worded affidavit in 1985. The absence of any mention of provenance puzzled all three previous potential buyers of the Cardona. On his website, the owner remained silent on these matters.

As for the question of authenticity, neither Stephen Colston's evaluation (a redacted part of which is also posted on the website), nor the Fox letter, nor the radiocarbon dating tests (one gives a date of 2045 BP plus or minus 50 years for the *amate* paper, and the other gives a result of "modern," or post-1945) directly support the Cardona's authenticity.

"For many years," the owner writes, "I took care of the codex and spent a considerable sum of money for tests and for the appropriate payment to expert evaluators." He doesn't say that the main purpose of the various evaluations was to authenticate the Cardona *for sale* in Britain and the United States. Moreover, I'd learned that the Getty had paid Colston, Stanford had paid the fee for the Crocker Lab's work and the carbon-14 tests, and Sotheby's of London had paid for a series of other examinations, including an opinion on the *amate* paper. And Thomas Schwarz had told me that he had spent a large amount of his own money on the project.

Finally, another strange document in the posting says that the Cardona was "delivered" (*entregado*) to the Museo de Historia Mexicana in Monterrey,

Mexico, in 1997. But barely a year later, as we shall see, the owner consigned the Cardona to three antiquities dealers for sale. Likewise, the owner had the Cardona registered by the Museum of Anthropology and History in Mexico City. Both of these acts were apparently done without fanfare, perhaps in silence, and did not involve any evaluation for authenticity. Were these acts designed to establish an aura of legitimate ownership?

With the nearly worthless and false "facts" out of the way, the Internet posting turns to an astonishing record of alleged deceit and betrayal on the part of Rivero Lake and his associates, and eventually to their alleged theft of the Cardona—though it's not at all clear who the specific thief was! The events in the posting, whether true or not, were apparently a last-ditch effort by the owner to regain control of the Cardona, thinking, apparently, that the Internet denunciation would shame the thief or thieves into returning the Cardona—just as, the owner apparently thought, Van Rijn's exposure had led Rivero Lake to return the Challapampa baroque altar to Peru. But let us turn to the codex owner's own words as posted on the website.

"Because of the importance of the document known as the Codex Cardona," the second part of the Internet posting begins, "there were many people interested in acquiring it or selling it for me." Among such people, the owner names a señora Velia Meade, who, along with a Spaniard named Pedro Saorín Box, a painter and Madrid antiquities dealer, contacted the owner, expressing their interest in the Cardona ("in this treasured document"), having been persuaded by "the antecedents regarding authenticity and origin."

The owner candidly admits that at this time he was passing through a difficult period, or more precisely, "difficulties that for various reasons of a personal nature beyond my control, had led to the loss of several millions of dollars." This admission squares with Ignacio Bernal's notion that Gutiérrez Esquivel had gotten in trouble with the Bank of Mexico with the consequent foreclosure on his properties and the threat of jail. But there may have been other difficulties as well. "Tempted by the reiterated offers from señora Meade and Pedro Saorín Box to sell the codex for me," the owner continues, "I agreed to consign the codex to them with the condition that the Cardona be sold only to a Mexican."

Presumably taking advantage of the owner's precarious financial situation, Meade and Saorín Box were able to drive down the amount they agreed to pay the owner to only $1.8 million. The owner accepted these terms but, given the delicacy of the transaction, insisted that two highly knowledge-able and trusted experts — "two specialists in these kinds of deals," "well-known to me" — come on board.

"Here," the owner ruefully reports, "is where the brothers Francisco and Rodrigo Rivero Lake became involved."

In the arrangement finally worked out, Meade and Saorín Box were to offer the Cardona for sale — "only to a Mexican" — for whatever amount they could obtain. From the proceeds of the sale, Meade and Saorín Box were to deliver $1.8 million to the owner, and the brothers Rivero Lake would re-ceive a $50,000 commission from the owner "for handling security." What-ever Meade and Saorín Box received above this amount was theirs to keep. This was, in effect, a fire sale; the owner was obviously desperate for cash.

The Internet posting then states that on October 6, 1998, the owner and his "employees" handed over the Codex Cardona to Rodrigo and Francisco Rivero Lake, who were parked in their car outside no. 395 calle Barrilaco, in the upper-class district of Lomas de Chapultepec. A few days later, the great map of Mexico-Tenochtitlán was also delivered to the brothers Rivero Lake, this time not in their parked car but to Rivero Lake's tenth-floor gallery in no. 199 Campos Elisios. The map had not been included in the original agreement. Remarkably, the exchange was carried out in the total absence of paperwork, with no receipts, no title of ownership, nothing; because, as the owner explains, he had been a client of Rivero Lake for many years, buying many important pieces in this same way, "a custom that in some cases prevails in transactions in Mexico City."

Thereafter the affair turned ugly. As the days and then months wore on, there was no apparent progress on the sale of the codex. On various occa-sions, the owner writes, "the Rivero Lake brothers informed me that every-thing was going 'marvelously well' and that in a very short time señora Velia Meade would have the money." Nevertheless, more excuses were made, along with new proposals for negotiation, and it seemed clear to the owner that Rodrigo Rivero Lake, Velia Meade, and Pedro Saorín Box were all in cahoots and not negotiating in his best interest. "In conversation with me," the owner states in the website posting, "they all gave similar evasive answers and seemed *nerviosísimos*."

Apparently because of the ever more urgent need for money to stave off his creditors, and his growing suspicion that things were not going well, the owner flew to New York City and found Rivero Lake ensconced in a small hotel off Central Park around the corner from the Plaza Hotel. Confronted by the owner, Rivero Lake delayed, claiming that he had a previous engagement. The two men agreed to meet two hours later.

Taking advantage of his forced wait, the owner, ever the *coleccionista*, took in the permanent Negroni exhibition of early modern European armor and weapons in the Metropolitan Museum of Art and returned to the hotel at the appointed hour. He claims that he waited two hours more for Rivero Lake to appear in the lobby, but even then, Rivero Lake could only provide "vague answers."

Though driven to desperation, the owner could do nothing but return to Mexico City. After a few days, perhaps faced with bankruptcy and even jail and learning that Rivero Lake had also returned to Mexico, the owner states that, accompanied by his son, he surprised Rivero Lake in his penthouse on Campos Eliseos, pushed past a gentleman holding the door, and demanded that the codex be returned. Then, according to the owner, "after the initial shock" of the unanticipated confrontation wore off, Rivero Lake gathered his composure, saying simply (in the familiar voice), "No te lo puedo dar": "I can't give it to you."

The owner does not record his reaction to this affront. In the Internet posting, the owner mulls bitterly over his fate, saying that Rivero Lake has no legal right to the codex, since it was never signed over to him; and besides, "taking a national treasure out of the country is a crime punishable under Mexican law as well as by international legislation." He cites a UNESCO ruling of 1970. Under these circumstances, "there is no way Rivero Lake could have obtained an export certificate unless there were other people involved." Here the owner, from his own previous experience in offering the codex to foreign buyers, must surely know what he's talking about.

Finally, the owner explains why he expressed his complaint on Van Rijn's website. "Despite having sought through mutual friends an arrangement with Rodrigo Rivero Lake," a proper resolution has not been possible. "He will respond to no demand except one that exposes him to public opinion." Apparently someone, perhaps the owner himself or an advisor, had seen Michel Van Rijn's successful exposure of Rivero Lake in the Cuzco altar case and decided to employ the same means.

So who carried the Codex Cardona to Christie's? We know it was there because Stephanie Wood saw it there in mid-November 1998. But we don't know who presented it to Christie's or gathered it up and disappeared after it was rejected by Christie's in May 1999. The owner reflects bitterly—perhaps disingenuously—that "whoever has it now probably doesn't know, or maybe doesn't care anything about questions of legality or authenticity or the improper transactions that brought it into his hands."

Not long after seeing the posting on the Van Rijn site, and taking advantage of a visit to my daughter in New York, I rang Christopher Coover at Christie's again, asking for an appointment in Manhattan. He was surprisingly friendly, more so than in my previous calls. He was in the middle of preparing for an elaborate auction, however, and could not see me until the following week. He said again, apologizing, that Christie's was not permitted to discuss the Codex Cardona file but that he would tell me, as he had before, who was *not* involved in the negotiations.

After the Internet posting, I had a few more names to run by him.

"Velia Meade," I asked.

"No."

"Pedro Saorín Box?"

"Nor him."

I held my breath before naming my prime suspect. "Rodrigo Rivero Lake?"

"No," Coover said, "none of those names was involved in our dealing with the Codex Cardona; and I don't really want to go beyond this. I'm sure you understand that we have to keep our files confidential."

CHAPTER FOURTEEN

The Architect's Studio

> Don Guillermo sat down suddenly, looked Andrés
> full in the face, and asked: "Do you want me to tell where
> I *really* got the Codex Cardona?"

 What reverberations had followed the owner's dramatic accusation on the Internet? What had Rivero Lake thought about this public denunciation? Glued to my computer screen, I found no new postings and no address through which I might contact the person who had written the account. I did find, however, an address for Mr. Van Rijn on his website, so on April 23, 2006, I sent off an e-mail to Amsterdam.

Dear Mr. Van Rijn:

I'm not sure how to get information from you or your website. My question is, do you have any more information available on the subject of the Codex Cardona, posted on your site, which connected Rodrigo Rivero Lake and the owner of the Codex Cardona? I have been interested in the Codex Cardona for several years.

Ten days later, I got an e-mail reply, not from Van Rijn but from one Luisa Andrade Rico, in English:

Michel van Rijn forwarded to me your address and asked me to establish contact with you regarding the Codex Cardona. Is there something you know that could add to the information found on Michel van Rijn's website? Even a small detail can be important.

With kind regards,
Luisa

I wrote back immediately to "Luisa" explaining that I'd seen the Cardona at the Crocker Lab many years ago, that I was a professor at the University of California, and that my interest was purely academic. I then mentioned that I was interested "in writing something" about the codex but might also have information that would interest her and that I would very much like to discuss my findings with the person who had put up the posting on the Van Rjin site. To put it this way did seem perhaps unnecessarily coy; but given the past secrecy surrounding the Cardona and my strong sense that a delicate touch was in order, it was no time for what might seem offensive presumption. I wondered if she might be able to put me in touch with the owner to arrange an appointment? I remarked that my several previous attempts to identify the owner had not been successful.

To this plea and subsequent follow-ups I received no reply. As days turned into weeks a sense of unease was followed by growing anxiety and then resignation. Did I imagine that the distinguished architect would respond to a request for an interview out of the blue from a gringo with an unknown agenda? To discuss sensitive information? Then, on July 12, Luisa wrote, in English:

"I would have liked to talk with you in Mexico City, but as far as the owner is concerned, he has not been well and will be unable to meet with you at this time. I am curious. What is your specific interest in the codex?"

Well, of course, the owner might really not be well, I thought. But he has other reasons for not talking with a North American who might bring up questions about authenticity, and worse, about his efforts to sell the codex in Britain and the United States. Or he might simply not have the time in what surely is a busy life. Then, too, I wondered, who is "Luisa"? A Mexican stringer for Van Rijn? A *confidante* of the owner?

I wrote back expressing my regrets that the owner was indisposed, and repeated my reasons for wanting to talk with him in person. I said again that I did have information that I thought would interest him and added, "Since it appears that you are in touch with the owner, can you please ask if a later date would be possible?" I feared that my remark about wanting to "write something" about the codex had spooked the owner.

I sent three follow-ups to my first message and had pretty much given up when, on August 17, I received an unexpected e-mail from Luisa Andrade.

Dear Professor—

It would be good to be able to talk with you in Mexico City. As far as the owner of the Codex, the Architect, don Guillermo Gutiérrez Esquivel, is concerned it also might be possible to arrange to see him. He has been unwell but is very interested in finding his Codex.

The reason she hadn't written sooner, she explained, was "that I was out of town. Besides, I also had a computer system crash."

Implausible, I thought, but before I could indulge my usual skepticism, Luisa wrote again.

Can you be in Mexico City on August the 23rd? I've just spoken with don Guillermo to confirm that date. We could meet at his studio in the street Porfirio Diaz 106, 4th Level at 1100 in the morning.

So there it was. After all this time, the person who had always loomed in the background of my search, the man I had sought and often suspected to be the owner, the man described by Thomas Schwarz as "a gentleman of Hispanic descent resident in London" and later, in the Getty and Stanford negotiations, as the "owner who wished to remain anonymous" — that man might now meet with me. After twenty years, Gutiérrez Esquivel had come forth: first in a desperate, anonymous, and not wholly truthful plea on Van Rijn's website, and now in agreeing to an interview with an obscure professor from California who stood to gain more than he could offer.

How could I not go to meet him? Maybe now my long search for the story of the Codex Cardona could be resolved. On the other hand, what could he possibly say that he hadn't already on the website? And what could I tell him that he didn't already know? After all, I didn't know where his codex was!

I looked up my young colleague Andrés Reséndez in his office to tell him the news. It turned out that he was already planning to visit his mother in Mexico City in late August, before the fall term began.

"Of course you have to go," Andrés said. "I'll be busy with my mother, but we can overlap at least one day. I'll go with you to see don Guillermo on the twenty-third. Maybe you'll need some protection," he added with a slightly nervous smile. "There are some dark characters in this story."

It would be another plunge into secrecy, half-truths, and deceptions, I thought. And I'd hate to be assaulted at seven thousand feet above sea level. That could cause a stroke. I'd heard of such cases. But, of course, I had to go. I handed over my credit card to Rosie at Travel Express. Maybe the end to my quest was in sight.

The airport taxi took me back again to the María Cristina, the place I've always stayed over the past half century whenever I come as a tourist to this noxious, fascinating, car- and crime-strangled city. It's a small hotel, four stories of terra-cotta colonial stucco with a quiet garden along one side with huge *fresno* trees, a manicured lawn, and bougainvillea spilling over an iron fence. Somehow the incessant roar of cars bumping over the potholes of Río Lerma Street doesn't penetrate the cool interior of tile and highly polished floors. An open staircase decorated with Talavera tile winds around the well-kept interior patios.

Adolfo Soriano, the day clerk, had worked at the María Cristina nearly as long as I'd been coming as a guest. Eyes on the ledger, he mumbled a grumpy something-or-the-other as I approached the desk. Then he looked up over his glasses, and, surprised, greeted me:

"Bienvenido, Señor. Back so soon. And the Señora?"

"She's sticking close to the hearth," I said.

"You're lucky she lets you get away."

I handed my bags and laptop to the porter and my credit card to Adolfo.

"How are the Mexicans?" I asked.

"Completely fucked," he said, "not the way we remember it from the days of Ruíz Cortínez and López Paseos." He repeated an old joke on the president's name, and I felt pleased knowing that he knew I'd get it.

"I love it," I said. "I always like to come back to Mexico. It takes me back to my green years." The salad days. Outside in the garden bar, I had a shot of *tequila reposado* cooled off with a Bohemia and some salty fried pumpkin seeds in honor of those former presidents when everything was better, and then I went to bed without supper.

The next morning, after the elevation and my high expectations had caused a near-sleepless night, I had a plate of ripe papaya and asked the hotel *taxista* the fare to the Parque Hundido, out on Insurgentes Sur, and then to Porfirio Díaz Street, number 106. I was to meet Andrés at 10:30 at the entrance to the building. Porfirio Díaz Street is relatively quiet, leafy with thin *truenos* and *liquidambar* on one side, the Sunken Park on the other. I got out of the taxi and walked past an attractive coffee place with small tables and a man inside bent over the espresso machine. Young people were reading; a benign sight.

Andrés hadn't arrived, so I struck up a desultory conversation with the uniformed young man out front of number 106, who seemed officially employed, though his precise tasks weren't obvious. I mentioned El Arquitecto. "Yes," the young man said, pointing to a steel-paneled wall with five call buttons, "he's on level four." I waited until 11:15, and then a bit more, and when Andrés didn't show, I pushed the button, identified myself on the intercom, took the elevator to the fourth floor, and rang another buzzer.

A handsome, well-dressed woman of around fifty answered the door and offered me her hand.

"I'm Cecilia Lemberger," she said in Spanish, "the same person as Luisa Andrade Rico. I use both names. But you can call me Cecilia." I must have looked surprised but then took this little twist in stride.

A slight, trim, straight-backed, handsome man—in California, one might even say beautiful—stood a few steps into the studio. His silver hair was combed back smoothly; he had a kindly face and expressive brown eyes. He seemed open, voluble, perhaps in his seventies, and was apparently in very good health. He wore elegant, expensive clothes: gray flannel trousers, shirt and tie, a tweed jacket. This was El Arquitecto, don Guillermo Gutié-rrez Esquivel. At last.

He came forward with a firm stride and offered his hand. It was a bright studio where light, even on a cloudy day, poured in through huge windows on three sides of the room. We introduced ourselves, and he motioned me to sit on a black leather sofa. He sat across from me on a low, heavy table of polished wood, leaning forward, almost elflike, his knees practically touching mine. On the table lay an unusual *mano* and *metate*, the rustic native Mesoamerican stones for grinding maize.

There was small talk. I told him I very much admired his work on the Franz Meyer. Something came up about oligarchies and democracy—because of the stalemated Mexican presidential elections and the street block-ades by the opposition—just then on everyone's mind. While we waited for Andrés, he began to show off early editions of old books, including a mid-seventeenth-century second edition of *Don Quixote*, various other artifacts from Spain, awards on framed parchment, sketches and picture albums of architectural works. He darted around the studio, carrying over to the sofa this object and that from different piles and shelves. I could only murmur my wonder and approval at this whirlwind of display, and I wished that An-drés would show up. What could have happened to him?

Don Guillermo was surrounded by what must have been the remnants of his once imposing collections. There were suits of armor, pikes, and swords—no wonder he was interested in the Negroni collection at the Met—crossbows, elegant Italian telescopes, statuary, an ancient wood crucifix, and modern sculpture, all displayed so that strategically placed mirrors illuminated all sides, creating strange illusions. His studio occupied the entire floor of a modern apartment building, and the ceiling was supported by a number of foot-square pillars encased in additional reflecting mirrors that turned the entire flat into a kind of oversized trompe l'oeil; much like my quest for the Cardona itself, I thought. Stuck to one of the windows with Scotch tape were blown-up slides that I later recognized as two of the Cardona's magnificent maps.

Around 11:30 Andrés arrived and took his place to my left on the sofa. Don Guillermo moved down the table to sit opposite him. I think we were all relieved that Andrés had come. I was getting the impression that don Guillermo could be described as a "Hispanist," a term applied a few decades ago to the older, conservative Catholic social stratum in Latin America that saw Spain as the source of its culture and considered the North Americans to be loud, wealthy, and barbarous, useful mainly for capital investment and as allies against social disorder among the lower classes. The Cold War, in fact, had forced the Hispanists, grinding their teeth every step of the way, into an alliance with the vulgar gringos to keep the communists at bay.

Maybe I was wrong about this, but while I found don Guillermo an enormously appealing man, he never really warmed up to me. Of course, this could have been for many reasons; comme on dit, there's no accounting for taste. He mentioned two or three times his father's birthplace, near Burgos in Spain, "in the very cradle of Castile," as he put it. In any case, whatever his social predilections, he was happy talking with Andrés, to whom he seemed to take an immediate liking. And no wonder; Andrés, as I'd thought when I met him at a recruitment dinner, and now seeing him in his own country, was a man of the sort I had become familiar with during my student days in Mexico City. He's highly intelligent with a special affability, at once alert and courteous, friendly and reserved—qualities that are much prized by educated Mexicans.

Cecilia was not easy to read. Who was she? What was her role in this encounter? Indeed, in the entire Cardona saga? She sat to my right in a matching black leather chair, quietly taking notes on a lined yellow pad. Now and then, distressed by don Guillermo's wandering monologue, she tried to get him back on track and even pointedly suggested that he might permit the visitors a word.

In the midst of don Guillermo's disconnected display of artifacts, catalogs, and models of hotels and houses he'd designed, I'd begun to fear that time would run out—I didn't know how much we had—and the thousand questions I had would never be addressed. So, during a brief opening in the conversation, I inserted the subject of the visit: our common interest in the Codex Cardona.

"You may wonder why we've come to your country, indeed to your house," I stiffly began, and launched into a formal rap about how I'd seen the actual codex twenty years ago, had followed its history, and now wanted to share my knowledge with señor Gutiérrez and—I nodded to Cecilia—with the señora. What we all wanted was to find the Codex Cardona. I felt my pulse speed up and the ringing swell in my ears. I felt I had to demonstrate my credentials, to show I was serious about the codex, but I had to get out of this high-in-the-chest, nervous talk. But how? Some hard information, perhaps? Interest them in things they might not know?

I was pleased with the connections my research on Blanco White, Felipe Neve, and the Jesuits had yielded, and thought those details might be interesting to don Guillermo and Cecilia; after all, El Arquitecto had repeated the Spanish connection on the Internet posting. I had barely begun when don Guillermo leaped to his feet, rummaged through a pile of loose papers, and handed around a stack of the working drawings he'd used for the restoration of the Franz Mayer Museum. This led to a lengthy discussion about the skeletons and crania they'd found several meters below ground level. This was a rude jolt. I thought he might be in an early stage of dementia. Or perhaps this was the "poor heart" Cecilia had alluded to in the e-mail? He seemed to have zero, but zero, interest in my information on the Cardona. Cecilia cast an annoyed glance at him, indicating that he should sit still.

Once things settled down again, I skipped from the Blanco White business to what I knew about the Cardona's appearance at Christie's. I was showing my cards without getting so much as a peek at theirs. But since Gutiérrez Esquivel's posting on the Van Rijn website had not mentioned Christie's, I thought he would welcome new information. I talked about my conversations with Chris Coover at Christie's—don Guillermo and Cecilia seemed not to know about Coover or to care about Christie's—and I even mentioned that a North American colleague had vetted the codex and that I'd seen her report. I revealed that Coover told me that he'd not heard of Velia Meade or Saorín Box or even of Rivero Lake. All of this seemed to fall on deaf, or at least indifferent, ears, apart from don Guillermo's mumbled remark, with a glance at Cecilia, that the Internet posting had been a mistake and that "those people—Meade and Saorín—are more of Rivero Lake's *rufianes.*" His own mention of Rivero Lake set don Guillermo off, and he repeated the story of the penthouse confrontation I'd read on the Internet.

I persisted with a few more clumsy attempts to draw out El Arquitecto and Cecilia on what they knew about the codex and then asked rhetorically, "Who, then, sold it? Where is it now?" And the questions I didn't ask: Where did it come from? And how did *you* acquire it? There was, I fear, amused interest in my candor, mixed with an edge of contempt, on don Guillermo's handsome face. He waved a hand dismissively. "Oh, they say it's been sold to an *hotelero* (a hotel man) in Barcelona." He then turned away from me toward Andrés.

I picked up on the tension between Cecilia and El Arquitecto and tried to move to safer ground, but not before she elaborated on don Guillermo's encounter with Rivero Lake in the penthouse apartment. "Actually," she said, "Guillermo went with his son, who managed to calm him down. There was some shoving and maybe a blow or two."

Don Guillermo brushed this off with another dismissive and exasperated gesture, saying that it was irrelevant. He later told us that he "was getting rid of that woman."

The mood subsided, and I asked Cecilia about the Universidad Metropolitana—where she'd said she worked—and then, since it was around 2:00, about places for lunch nearby.

"It's the season for *chiles en salsa nogada*," she said. "There's a good place not far, La Poblanita."

I mentioned the Hostería Santo Domingo, which she dismissed as being too far, and the San Angel Inn as too expensive. Speaking of food, and since I was free on Friday, I asked if she'd like to have lunch. Cecilia had been my main contact in arranging an appointment with Gutiérrez Esquivel, and I thought she might tell me more about the circumstances leading to the Internet posting—it was obvious now that she had put it up—and other information that we were not going to get in the company of don Guillermo. We agreed that I'd call her on Friday.

Meanwhile I dimly heard Andrés and don Guillermo talking about the color slides of the codex. So they are here, I thought, not with Tonatiuh. At least that mystery is solved. Andrés involved me in this discussion, and we talked about finding a way to publish some or all of the slides so that there would be a public record of this magnificent document even if the original were never found. Always thinking first about money, I remembered how publishing the four-volume luxury edition of the Codex Mendoza had practically bankrupted the University of California Press, and I made some cautious remarks about such a project, the difficulty in transcribing the paleography, of finding expert commentary, and the necessity of financial support. How boring of me, I thought; this is old men's talk. In contrast, don Guillermo and Andrés had become animated, very enthusiastic about such a project.

To my astonishment, Andrés then suggested to don Guillermo that he and I take the slides to California, copy them onto a high-quality CD, and in a month return the slides and a copy of the disc to don Guillermo. And, of course, we would do nothing with them without his strict approval. El Arquitecto was enthusiastic about that as well, although I could hardly believe my ears. Cecilia was shocked. She stood up abruptly.

"I'm shocked, shocked," she said. "Guillermo, this is *not* a good idea."

Don Guillermo dismissed her objections with an imperious sweep of his hand. He agreed with Andrés on the need for an inventory and that we should return to the studio after lunch.

We took the elevator down and grabbed a taxi off the street, trying, as the driver rocketed through the traffic on Insurgentes, to imagine the conversation going on between El Arquitecto and Cecilia.

The San Angel Inn was packed even on a weekday. We sat in the patio of this delightful place, long a favorite, waiting for a table. Margaritas appeared in small, ice-cold silver vases. I never drink margaritas; but celebration was in order. Andrés and I both had the *chile en salsa nogada*, and a flan and *café exprés* afterward, while going over the remarkable events of the morning, not knowing that we were in for another and greater surprise in the afternoon.

Cecilia did not return to the studio after lunch, and don Guillermo made no mention of her absence. From a formidable Fire Star safe, he produced a box—the original box, with label and stamps, addressed to señor Tonatiuh Gutiérrez, calle Belisario Domínguez 68, from Thomas Schwarz, 738 South Bristol, Santa Monica, California. How extraordinary that the slides I had talked about with Colston, Olsberg, and Wim de Wit at the Getty could be found in their original box in Mexico, now being handed over to us by Guillermo Gutiérrez Esquivel. The slides were like distant relatives I'd never met but now was curious to see.

Andrés sat down at a large draftsman's table and began sorting through the slides. In a bit, after don Guillermo had stopped ricocheting around the room, offering running commentary on a variety of random subjects, he sat down suddenly, looked Andrés full in the face, and asked:

"Do you want me to tell where I *really* got the Codex Cardona?"

Was I hearing this right? Was this a confession? Andrés stopped sorting slides, not knowing quite what to say except something like "Yes, well, please do."

Don Guillermo told us that some twenty years ago, more or less, he'd come across a rare book and antiquities dealer named Enrique Medina in a winding, block-long row of antiquities dealers in the so-called Zona Rosa of Mexico City, the center of Mexico City's tourist district. Don Guillermo had noticed a small, disorderly stack of what appeared to be sixteenth-century documents, perhaps a dozen, "just lying on the floor." He bought these, he said, for a good price, returned in the following weeks and months as more became available, and finally made an agreement to buy whatever the dealer could get his hands on.

"As I got more of them, I saw that they formed a coherent whole with pages numbered in sequence. I was the first person to notice this and continued to buy everything Medina acquired. You could say that I rescued the Codex Cardona from ruin."

Over the course of two or three years, don Guillermo told us, he acquired over four hundred pages, including the many painted illustrations and the maps—he pointed to the prints he had taped to the window—"that you see photographs of there." He didn't know, he said, whether Medina was getting the folios page by page or whether he had acquired the entire codex and was, for whatever reason, perhaps price, parceling them out in small batches. Don Guillermo added that the price of each additional page certainly went up.

"Actually," he added expansively, "I bought the pages from Medina in partnership with Tonatiuh Gutiérrez—no relation to me, by the way. We made an agreement when he was dying four or five years ago that thirty percent of the proceeds of any sale of the Cardona would go to his widow, Electra."

Andrés asked if Electra lived in Mexico. Don Guillermo said she'd moved to Spain shortly after Tonatiuh's death, which corroborated my friend Víctor Lomelí's information. Don Guillermo spoke fondly of Tonatiuh, saying that they had been very close, had both been *coleccionistas*, and had thought alike in many ways. I was still surprised that Schwarz would make up that story about "staying in touch" with Electra in Mexico when now it seemed she was actually in Spain. Perhaps Schwarz had confused the dates.

Andrés and I were transfixed, listening practically open-mouthed as don Guillermo spun out this new version. If true, it scrambled many of my previous leads and completely changed other antecedents and explanations that I'd been following, not to mention the elaborate false trail laid by the notarized affidavit from Madrid, or even don Guillermo's own recent account on Van Rijn's website.

"But where" — I managed to get out the first obvious question — "did the dealer, Enrique Medina, get the codex in the first place?"

"He didn't say," don Guillermo answered. "There was some talk of Indian communities nearby, here in the Valley of Mexico, maybe the town of Milpa Alta; but I'm not sure. In any case, I saw immediately that it was a priceless document that no one had previously noticed, and I was determined to acquire the entire codex." He jumped up and grabbed a magnifying glass to show us again the enlarged slide of the Coyoacán map. "Here, see. This shows the houses of Nuño de Guzmán and of don Hernán Cortés. The houses are now buried, of course, under other buildings; but with this map, they could be excavated. Everyone knows the house of La Malinche — it's still there — but never has there been a map so detailed of a mid-sixteenth-century town." He then casually mentioned that he'd lent some of the slides to someone — more dismissive gestures — for copying, and quite a few had been missing when the young man returned them. Don Guillermo seemed to be accustomed to being ripped off. Ignacio Bernal had also mentioned that El Arquitecto, "as he began to decline economically and emotionally, had many people around who were not exactly devoted to helping him."

We went back to the drawing board — literally, that is — and sat down. Andrés's anxiety level was rising fast because he was leaving on a night flight and still had half the slides to inventory. The new revelations raised a thousand questions, but it was already 6:00, and with the traffic there would be a terrific rush to get to his mother's house out in Ciudad Satélite, pick up his two small children, and still make the flight to San Francisco. We fell silent, Andrés furiously making notes about the slides, don Guillermo wandering off, fondly examining favorite objects from his *colecciones*, the ones, I reminded myself, that he'd previously kept in the Palacio del Marqués in Chiconcuac. Around 7:30 Andrés gathered up the slides and his inventory and notes, and we made our formal farewells.

"Oiga, listen," don Guillermo said, turning to me at the elevator. "I can take you to see Enrique Medina tomorrow, Thursday, and you can ask him about the documents. That would be a good day, better than Saturday, when those places are crowded. I'll come by your hotel at noon, and we can walk to his place."

"You don't have to bother, especially in this traffic; you can give me the address, and I can find the place."

"No, no," he graciously insisted. "It's no bother. I want you to meet him. I know your hotel, the one in Río Lerma."

Outside it was pouring rain, with incredible blasts of lightning and rolling thunder that seemed to detonate just over our heads. Andrés clutched the box of slides inside his raincoat and whistled for a passing taxi.

"Not off the street!" I protested. "Good god, we've got the only record, the only copy, of the Codex Cardona there is!"

"If we don't rush, I'll never make my flight—we'll pick a taxi that looks respectable!"

The car inched up the Avenida Insurgentes. We were as giddy as two teenagers after the senior prom as we tried to process what had happened during the day from beginning to end. The new twists at every turn in don Guillermo's tale made the story much more complicated.

"So what does it all mean?" I wondered aloud. We both nearly collapsed in laughter as the absurd possibilities washed over us. The entire day had a sense of weird unreality starting with Luisa/Cecilia's double name. Then, in the early discussion, every time we edged into fact, El Arquitecto had skated off into bizarre distractions, smoke screens, and off-the-mark information.

"So," Andrés began, "there's the curious relationship between Luisa/Cecilia and don Guillermo. Who is she? You were talking to her."

"Well, she was apparently the one who put up the Internet posting. That's all I know. She said she and don Guillermo are friends. There was something about her having a position in the Universidad Metropolitana. Maybe she's his mistress? She's pretty sharp-tongued; she talks to him like a *wife*, not like a friend."

"Did I miss something," I went on, "or isn't don Guillermo really scattered, losing a little something? I cannot, *cannot believe* that he handed over the slides to us! Without any paperwork! It's like the Rivero Lake transaction, redux. Now when he comes to California looking for them, we can say, 'No te las podemos dar!' I think he'll wake up tomorrow outraged.

Maybe he'll send the Judicial Police after *me*. You'll be gone, but they'll leap out of their black Ford Falcons and grab me!"

"I don't know," Andrés said. "El Arquitecto seemed enthusiastic about publishing the slides. Remember, too, that I told him that we'd do nothing without his approval."

"Yeah, but he has no reason to trust us. We just walked in off the street."

The taxi driver weaved, braked, changed lanes abruptly, and roared through a caution light, shaking his fist, all the while calmly assuring us that we'd make it on time. Andrés and I went on with our recap. Apart from everything else, the business about Medina had certainly enriched, but at the same time certainly cast into doubt, my narrative. Someone—supposing that Gutiérrez Esquivel was now telling the *real* truth—had laid out all these false trails at Sotheby's and the Getty about the Cardona's original owner being a "sixteenth-century Spanish nobleman." If the Enrique Medina story *was* true, someone had planted the entire elaborate Blanco White affidavit business, the connection with "Baron von Schultzenberg-León," and cooked up a story about the owner being a "person of Hispanic descent resident in London." And I, with unsuspecting credulity, had followed the scent, eagerly sniffing my way down a marked path all the way to the Firestone Library at Princeton—a path that, as it turned out, led into ever more unclear destinations. And what about Barlow? Does this give a death blow to any possibility of fraud?

Then, too, there's the Internet posting. Gutiérrez Esquivel had surely known what Cecilia put up, since the "facts" were his account, written in the first person. So if he hadn't been telling the truth to her, why think that he was now? And no wonder, I complained, that he had no interest in listening to my "historical antecedents" involving Felipe Neve or my information about the appearance at Christie's. It's as if he had known all about that, was far ahead of us in the account.

Then the story about Enrique Medina. "Are we to think," asked Andrés, "that Gutiérrez Esquivel never even *asked* Medina where the documents came from?"

"And the piecemeal purchase," I put in. "How would that have worked? Are we to believe that an Indian village official, from, say, Milpa Alta, trekked over to the Zona Rosa every couple of weeks during a two- to three-year period carrying a few sixteenth-century folios to Medina each time? It doesn't make any sense. It's more likely that the source was intermediaries—antiquities dealers or their agents—who search out rare documents in those communities. Or more likely still that Medina bought the entire codex and then parceled the pages out to Gutiérrez Esquivel, raising the price once he saw that El Arquitecto and Tonatiuh were hooked."

"Wouldn't don Guillermo, after he saw the codex was an integral work, have become anxious that Medina might sell some of the pages to someone else? He doesn't strike me as a patient man," Andrés added.

"Or," I said, "maybe the *tlahcuilos* in Milpa Alta were only able to forge eight or ten pages each week!"

"Under 'Barlow's' direction!" Andrés added with a sly smile. "In any case, don Guillermo is going to take you to Enrique Medina tomorrow. You can ask him all these questions."

CHAPTER FIFTEEN

Pasaje de las Flores

"Go along Londres here for three or four streets to El Pasaje
de las Flores. There you can find anything you're looking for."
Why that wink, I wondered?

 On Thursday I woke early and went across the street to buy copies of *La Jornada* and *La Reforma*. I had the usual plate of papaya and a *pan dulce* for breakfast, after which I sank down in one of the deep, uncomfortable sofas in the lobby and read my newspapers. Around ten o'clock I received a long-distance call that I took in the special booth behind the desk. It was Andrés calling from his house in California.

"You were right," he said. "El Arquitecto rang me a half hour ago, very agitated, worried about his slides and about us. He wanted me to bring the slides back from California immediately, and in the meantime he wants to bring over a formal receipt for you to sign this morning. I should also tell you that he thinks you've not been straight with him, that you're plotting, or something is going on, because you invited Cecilia to lunch. And he thinks you dissemble by feigning deafness!"

"That's a new one," I said. "In fact, I pretend to understand things I don't. I can cancel the lunch with Cecilia; it's for tomorrow."

"Anyway, he's in a state. I tried to calm him down, told him we were both *honrados*, and that I'd personally bring back the slides once they're digitized. That seemed to mollify him, but don't be surprised if he doesn't show up this morning."

This was depressing news, not just because don Guillermo was freaking out but because I liked him, felt kindly toward him, and was thrilled to meet him—and I hate to think that anyone would distrust me. Then, too, I was certainly looking forward to meeting Enrique Medina.

I waited in the lobby of the María Cristina from noon until 12:45, but don Guillermo didn't show. Lunch, what about lunch? I could now indulge myself with my favorite number for dining: two, oneself and the headwaiter. I remembered a place, La Fonda del Refugio, once really good, perhaps now touristy. I walked across the broad Avenida de la Reforma, which was blocked by the tents that political protesters had set up in the middle of the street. The tents were pretty much abandoned. Stuffed-cloth dummies on chairs had replaced the protesters, and a couple of homeless people were sleeping under blankets on the sidewalk. I would be early to La Fonda, so I decided to try to find Enrique Medina on my own. Don Guillermo had mentioned the streets of Londres and Hamburgo. Both were long streets running parallel to the Reforma with some fancy boutiques and restaurants, nice espresso places, and bookstores. In the seventies, this had been the glittering center of Mexico's tourist industry, but now it had pockets of tacky fast-food taco and burrito places, such as a garish Tacos y Enchiladas Brownsville.

I stepped into a tobacco store and asked if there might be antique or rare book stores in the neighborhood. "No que yo sepa," the young woman said, "not that I know." The third inquiry yielded a "Yes, go along Londres here for three or four blocks to El Pasaje de las Flores. There you can find anything you're looking for." Why that wink, I wondered?

El Pasaje de las Flores turned out to be an undulating interior mall running for a long block between two main streets, with expensive antique and rare book showrooms tucked away in individual *locales*. I walked the length of the passage and back again, wondering which one might be Enrique Medina's. The proprietors' names were not displayed. I chose Antiguedades Nuevo Mundo to inquire. The first two rooms out front were packed with polished colonial furniture, tapestries, *retablos*, paintings, arms and armor, medieval halberds, ornate lamps, crucifixes. A step down through an open door, a man was bent over a computer in the back room. He rose, somewhat reluctantly, as I tapped on the doorframe.

"Buenas tardes, señor. I wonder if by chance you might know if one could find in this Pasaje a gentleman by the name of Enrique Medina?"

The man gave me a sideways look, sizing me up. He was perhaps fifty, maybe older, well-preserved, handsome, with dark hair slicked back over his head.

"I am Enrique Medina, *a sus órdenes*."

No, it can't be, I thought, some sort of miracle. The one store I go into? I later walked though the Pasaje again, counting sixty-seven different *locales*. Señor Medina must have thought someone had given me the name of his store, but he didn't ask. We struck up a conversation about old books; I asked about colonial documents. He brought out a few official-looking things from the eighteenth century. I leafed though them and said I was more interested in the sixteenth. No, he said, he didn't have any at this time; they were very scarce. "Some years ago I had a stack" — he held out his hand to indicate a pile a couple of feet high — "but I haven't had any since."

Time was short, so I took a chance. "Were those by chance the ones that were acquired by El Arquitecto, señor Gutiérrez Esquivel?" "Sold," or "purchased," I thought, might be threatening verbs.

Who is this gringo? Medina must have wondered. But caught by surprise, he simply said, "Yes, he carried them away [*se los llevó*], as did other persons." It wasn't that Medina became unfriendly, but my abruptness and my unexpected query created distance. He didn't have to answer these questions from a stranger; besides, of course, the conversation had edged into delicate legal terrain. There was a bit more polite talk. I thanked him and expressed my admiration again for his collections. Then I walked through the Pasaje to Liverpool Street, made casual inquiries in other antiquity *locales* about colonial documents, and went on to La Fonda del Refugio. After the startling coincidence of finding Enrique Medina right off the bat, I had to sit down to gather my thoughts. Medina would not be back in Antiguedades Nuevo Mundo until after four o'clock. But first, the menu and specials of the day.

During my student days in Mexico City there were lots of fancy European-style restaurants, but proper Mexican cooking was hard to find outside private kitchens; there were only the endless cheap taco and torta streetside stands. Then regional dishes began to appear in Mexico City. Restaurateurs saw that given the chance, the mounting flood of visitors actually liked real Mexican cooking, and so the wonderful *moles* — the Nahuatl word for sauces — such as *pipián*, *poblano*, the *mole negro* from Oaxaca, and all kinds of other dishes, large and small, caught on, and delicious new places sprang up.

La Fonda del Refugio was one of these: a tourist place with excellent food. I was happy to see that it was still here. I started with two exquisite *chalupitas* and moved on to the *barbacoa* — lamb slow-cooked in maguey leaves—with *mole verde*. The tortillas were the ones I remembered: white and hot, not like the tasteless cardboard rounds you get in the United States. Why, I wondered, were the tortillas always hot and the coffee cold in Mexico and the other way around in the States? The Bohemia came in chilled mugs, and then *café de olla*. The only trouble was that I couldn't linger, so I raced through lunch. I had unfinished business with Enrique Medina.

This time señor Medina was standing just inside the main door. He didn't seem surprised that I had come back. I asked again about the sixteenth-century documents that Gutiérrez Esquivel and "otras personas" had "carried away." One of these persons, I figured, must have been Tonatiuh. Medina, with a furtive sideways glance, quite easily took up the subject of codices and old manuscripts. He said that the pages I mentioned made up an entire codex that included extremely valuable maps and illustrations. He didn't say that he'd sold the pages in installments. We talked at some length about sixteenth-century material, and then he asked:

"So whatever happened to that codex? Where is it now?"

"It was stolen," I said. "No one knows where it is."

Medina was surprised and even skeptical about this, so I suggested he go to his computer and click up "un códice es mucho más . . ." on the Internet. When he saw the section describing the previous owner of the Cardona as "a descendant of a sixteenth-century Spanish nobleman," who had sold it to "Baron von Schultzenberg-León," Medina pointed a finger at the screen and said, "Esto es una mentira": "This is a lie."

Our conversation began to take on a more mutually interested and even friendly tone. I asked Medina if he knew Rivero Lake—who, of course, appears as the thief in the website posting—and Medina said that he did. "Everyone does; but I don't think he's a thief."

I was trying to figure out the timing of Medina's transactions with Gutiérrez Esquivel, so I asked him when El Arquitecto had acquired the codex.

"It must have been eighteen or twenty years ago," he said.

That agreed with don Guillermo's recollection.

It was now 2006. A rapid calculation told me that since the Cardona had been offered to Sotheby's in early 1982, and since Gutiérrez Esquivel said he had purchased the codex in installments over a two- to three-year period, Medina had to have begun the installment sales at least twenty-eight years ago. I pointed this out.

"Well, it might have been earlier," he said.

But then how old would Medina have been twenty-eight years ago, in

1978 or 1979? If, say, he was fifty now, he would have been twenty-two or twenty-three, an unusually young age for an established antiquities dealer. Moreover, would he have mistaken by nearly a decade the date of his sale to don Guillermo? Would they both have? It was possible, I thought, but a tad suspicious.

I tried gingerly to turn the talk to the codex's origins. "The sixteenth-century stuff is rare," I said, "I imagine hard to find. Where, may I ask, do these things come from? Where do you get these kinds of old papers in the first place?"

"De los pueblos," Medina said, with an encompassing wave of his hand, "from the Indian communities here in the Valley of Mexico. They're kept by the town councils or even in individual houses for centuries, and now and then—very rarely—they turn up. Usually the federal government or INAH, the National Institute of Anthropology and History, snaps them up, and the pueblos never see them again. Or dishonest INAH officials get their hands on them. INAH is in charge of the great museum along the Reforma, which I'm sure you're familiar with, and of all the archaeological sites."

I indiscreetly murmured something about international conventions regulating the sale of cultural property.

He swept his hand in a low arc, parallel with the floor. "They just deal with things down there," he said, "below ground."

As Medina talked about Indian communities—*comunidades cerradas*, or "closed communities," as he called them, using a now out-of-date designation—I remembered Stephanie Wood telling me that she'd recently seen a beautiful sixteenth-century manuscript that had come out of a village in Oaxaca, brought to the Burgos Library for restoration. And then I recalled— strange how the memory works—a long essay by the Mexican writer Carlos Fuentes about his interview with a peasant leader in the state of Morelos, just south of Mexico City. Developers were trying to take over the village lands, and Fuentes and some of his city friends had turned out to express their solidarity. Not to worry, the *campesino* said, "no coman ansias," don't feed on anguish. He went into his house and brought out a steel box, carefully taking out the titles to the village's common lands. King Phillip II, he claimed, had signed the papers. Fuentes had written about how the *campesino* must have thought that justice could be founded on that holy bit of parchment signed by a king of old—the same Spanish monarch, it occurred to me, to whom the Codex Cardona should have been sent in the mid-sixteenth century. Now it seemed pretty clear that he never got it.

It wasn't impossible that the Codex Cardona could have been tucked away for 450 years in an Indian community; and then, for whatever reason, a peasant leader or a shrewd friend might have persuaded the village elders to try to sell the documents in Mexico City. Medina couldn't, or more understandably didn't want to, go much beyond his original explanation. He couldn't, or wouldn't, name the Indian community. Gutiérrez Esquivel had offhandedly mentioned Milpa Alta, but when I suggested this to Medina, it didn't ring a bell. Nor, he said, could he recall the name of the person who had originally brought him the old papers. "After all," he said again, "this took place at least twenty years ago." Not wanting to be indelicately personal, I restrained myself from asking how old he was now.

There were holes in Medina's and Gutiérrez Esquivel's otherwise plausible stories that, at this remove in time, may be impossible to fill. The unnamed village, if there was one, has very likely been swallowed up by the uncontainable expansion of one of the planet's largest cities, its citizens silently absorbed by Mexico City or Los Angeles, California. Moreover, and understandably enough, Enrique Medina would not be inclined to go further in his discussion of the codex's origins. Whoever acquired the documents from an Indian *comunidad*, as well as the person who bought them, was acting on the margins of the law—if the papers were publicly brought to light, they might be confiscated by the Mexican authorities and, in principle at least, placed in national archives or museums.

And the dates weren't right. Both Medina and Gutiérrez Esquivel were a decade off in their memories. Moreover, if Gutiérrez Esquivel and Tonatiuh had seen immediately that the loose papers formed a coherent and consequently a valuable whole, would they have sat around patiently for the entire 427 pages to show up in small batches in Enrique Medina's store over a two- to three-year period? Then, once the codex was complete, why rush to Sotheby's in London to sell it? Don Guillermo and Tonatiuh were *coleccionistas*, not traffickers, in art. And the affidavit? And Baron von Schultzenberg-León? What creative person would have concocted those tales? The codex may well have come from Milpa Alta or some other *comunidad cerrada*—or perhaps had been created there sometime during the past few decades by a "Robert Barlow" or some other extraordinarily knowledgeable but impecunious scholar. In Barlow's day, the 1940s, expert *tlahcuilos* were more common than they are now. There was no smoking *pistola*, no proven account of the Cardona's history during the 430 years between its presumed creation in the 1550s and 1982.

Finally, it occurred to me that almost all the old papers found in Indian communities pertain to land titles or lawsuits in that specific community and might well be kept by the community for centuries. But the compilation of the Codex Cardona had been ordered personally by the viceroy of Mexico and supervised by a crown officer, Alonzo Cardona y Villaviciosa. Such official work, carried out at the highest bureaucratic level, was usually sent to Spain, as we've seen in the cases of the Codex Mendoza and the Telleriano-Remensis. How would a work such as the Cardona have ended up in an indigenous community? Among all the many explanations for the Cardona's origin, the one that has it emerging from an Indian village around 1980 hardly seemed more persuasive than the others.

As we left the store, Medina bent down to fasten the bottom lock of the heavy glass door to his *local*. He looked up at me.

"I didn't sell all the pages of the codex. I still have about thirty left, but not here. Maybe you'd like to buy them?"

"I doubt that I could afford them," I said. Then I remembered that Stephen Colston had said in his report to the Getty that the Codex Cardona was incomplete: some thirty pages were missing.

CHAPTER SIXTEEN

The High End

Rivero Lake moves in the highest social and political circles of
Mexico. If you want something ancient and beautiful, not to
mention valuable, he's the man to see.

DANIEL I. MCCOSH, "Mexican Antiquario"

 I'd first heard of Rodrigo Rivero Lake from Ignacio Bernal
in the Librería Zócalo; and then, of course, he was named in
Gutiérrez Esquivel's Internet posting, which suddenly made
Rivero Lake a major player in the story of the Cardona. But
could he really have collaborated in the theft of Gutiérrez Esquivel's beloved
codex? Why? Well, dollars, of course; perhaps several million dollars. But
why the Cardona, and why steal from El Arquitecto, and why then? After all,
they were both collectors, had common interests, and had bought and sold
for each other for thirty years. Yet the dramatic account written by Gutiérrez Esquivel or dictated to Cecilia and posted on Michel van Rijn's website
seemed persuasive. Why would Gutiérrez Esquivel — or Cecilia — invent such
a story? That day in his studio, in a photo album that don Guillermo showed
me, I also saw an old snapshot of Rivero Lake, taken in happier times, in
the entrance to the Hacienda Chiconcuac. Under the picture, someone had
recently scrawled "El Ladrón" — the thief.

So who was Rodrigo Rivero Lake? Like most of us, he's no doubt many
people. I found an admiring account of a visit to Rivero Lake's gallery
and apartment in Campos Elisios Street in the wealthy neighborhood of
Polanco.

"Rivero Lake moves in the highest social and political circles of Mexico,"
the piece begins. "If you want something ancient and beautiful, not to mention valuable, he's the man to see. Once off the elevator to Rivero Lake's

penthouse apartment overlooking Mexico City's Chapultepec Park, visitors navigate down a hallway through a tightly packed collection of antique furniture, paintings and architectural pieces. It's like entering a combination museum and warehouse."

"At the end of the hallway," the article continues, "is a vacant bench that acts as a waiting area and it is there that we met Rivero Lake, a highly energetic if somewhat disheveled man who appeared clad only in socks, one black and the other grey." Only in socks? I wondered.

The account continues: "It is this mix of irreverence and respect for history that defines Rivero Lake as one of the last of the dying breed of 'field antiquarians.'"[1] Rivero Lake is also described as Mexico's "most well-known and prestigious antiquities dealer . . . a person with close connections in the banking and corporate world . . . who enjoys protection and even immunity in judicial matters . . . to cross him may be injurious to your health." "No charges," the writer adds, "have ever been successfully carried out against him up to now, at least, in Mexico."

The Mexican social pages often show Rivero Lake dining with writers and artists, and in one of the society magazines I saw a photograph of him dining with the American representative of Christie's of New York. In an interview in January 2006, Rivero Lake spoke about his new book on Namban art and about his recent travels in Italy and Spain, "researching, buying and selling antiquities."[2]

Described as "the most famous antiquarian in Mexico," Rivero Lake is a respected expert in many fields, especially in Asian art and its influence on colonial America, and a well-known author who displays his opinion at international and local meetings. Indeed, I later read that on the day when Andrés and I had visited Gutiérrez Esquivel's studio, Rivero Lake had been in Puebla, participating in an officially sponsored conference at the famed Palafox Library.

In addition to Gutiérrez Esquivel's allegations about the theft of the Codex Cardona, at about the same time, Rivero Lake had been involved in several other negotiations that had aroused suspicion. In 2000 thieves cut from its frame a seventeenth-century canvas, *Expulsion from the Garden of Eden*, in a church in the Mexican state of Hidalgo. In a matter of months, the painting was acquired by the San Diego Museum of Art. This had occurred "despite strict Mexican laws," solemnly declared the *San Diego Union-Tribune*'s staff writer in August 2006, "that provide little leeway for exporting Spanish Colonial art." A museum curator, however, became suspicious and alerted U.S. officials, who found that "the stolen painting was linked to Rodrigo Rivero Lake, a well-known art dealer and expert." The reporter added that no charges had been filed against Rivero Lake in Mexico, but the painting was eventually returned to Mexico. The *New York Times* reported this in a long story but did not mention the name of the "Mexico City dealer."[3]

A second, more spectacular theft of cultural property, as we've seen, had occurred earlier, involving the removal of eight murals depicting a "celestial choir" from the ceiling of a chapel in a seventeenth-century Peruvian hacienda near the highland capital of Cuzco. Somehow the panels passed illegally, but with no apparent difficulty, through two customs checks for reassembly in Mexico. Ten years later, in 2004, the Episcopal Commission for the Cultural Assets of the Church and Mariana Mould de Pease of the National Cultural Institute accused Rodrigo Rivero Lake—then the president of the Mexico City Sacred Art Commission—of having overseen the extraction of the ceiling murals and illegally shipping them to Mexico. This followed an allegation that Rivero Lake had previously stolen a baroque altarpiece and sold it in the United States. These cases and others publicized on the Van Rijn website led señora Mould de Pease to label Rivero Lake a "cultural predator." Responding in a long interview, Rivero Lake, barely able to contain his wrath at the very mention of Van Rijn's name, pointed out that "my job is to sell antiquities and I wouldn't be in Polanco, in Mexico City, in plain view for everyone, if I were not on the up and up. I document all my sales."

Far from "stealing" sacred art, he explained, "I save it. In Peru I saved it from the depredation of terrorist groups like the Shining Path who came through the Cuzco province burning churches and haciendas. And in Mexico I rescue objects from the 'brutal destruction' carried out by Evangelicals. When a community decides to change religion, the first thing they think about is burning down the Catholic churches. Van Rijn says he wants to preserve religious art; so do I. And that's what I *do*."

"In fact," he continued, "I've devoted 35 years of my life rescuing Mexican art and saving it *for Mexicans*. And another thing: if something is offered on the Internet, how am I to know if it's been stolen or not; how am I to know if an object has disappeared in some illicit way? Suppose someone finds a work of art, buys it and brings it to Mexico City to save it? Should I not buy it?"[4]

A few months earlier, in a generous gesture—or perhaps because his nemesis, Michel van Rijn, had plastered the issue of the altarpiece and the ceiling mural thefts all over his website—Rivero Lake was moved to return the altarpiece to Peru. The effect of negative publicity on Rivero Lake did not go unnoticed in Mexico City: as we've seen, it apparently inspired Gutiérrez Esquivel to post his allegations regarding the theft of the Codex Cardona on Van Rijn's site.[5]

It was also clear from the extensive Internet coverage that the record of Michel van Rijn, the implacable critic of the man he called "Lake the Snake," was hardly above reproach. Van Rijn had previously been an art dealer and smuggler. In his twenties, he sold a Rembrandt self-portrait by posing as a direct descendant of the seventeenth-century painter (who, in fact, had died without leaving any legitimate children). At thirty-seven, Van Rijn confessed in a documentary film, *The Artworld Dodger*—with his enemies and the law closing in—that he had agreed to become a police informant; later he transformed himself into a zealous, self-styled crusader dedicated to revealing art frauds and exposing the illicit acquisition of cultural patrimony. On January 22, 2005, the Swiss police arrested Van Rijn in Basel for alleged blackmail and in October 2006 Google removed his website. As the documentary filmmaker discovered in trying to figure out what made this extraordinary character tick, "it's hard to know what to believe from a man who's made a fortune from falsehood."[6]

It's also true that people in the art and antiquities world place a high value on authenticity, perhaps especially today, in our age of relative truth, when hardly anything is as it seems. The high price tag for authenticity is also fascinating to the general public, especially when tangled with crooked dealing beneath a veneer of respectability.

With the dramatic revelations Gutiérrez Esquivel had posted on Van Rijn's website, and now that I was seeing Rivero Lake's name, pictures, books, and the controversies about him all over the Internet, the renowned Mexico City dealer in antiquities had become for me, if not exactly a mythical figure, at least an exotic one. More than one person, talking to me about Rivero Lake, had cautioned me to be careful. I couldn't imagine that anyone would find a gray-haired, slightly limping gringo professor a threat. But still, if someone has the Judicial Police—the abusive and feared Judiciales— at his beck and call, well, things *can* happen. Moreover, in warning me away from an encounter with Rivero Lake, Andrés pointed out that if we could believe El Arquitecto's Internet posting, Rivero Lake had apparently stolen the Cardona. It wasn't likely that he was going to confess and tell me where the codex was!

I screwed up my courage and e-mailed Rivero Lake on September 2, 2006, saying simply that I was a historian of colonial Spanish America, that I would like very much to exchange information with him, *siempre que le conviniera*—as long as he found that suitable. I was surprised when Rivero Lake replied immediately:

"Soy su esclavo—I AM YOUR SLAVE. Tell me when and where and permit me to invite you to dine." Then, in more full caps, "I AM AT YOUR ORDERS!"

My slave? That was unexpected. Perhaps it fit with the picture of him as irreverent and disheveled—dressed only in unmatched socks.

The e-mail continued, "I didn't know about you!! What a shame. It's important to deal with 'gente investigatora y positiva!!'"

Positive researchers? And again in all caps:

"PLEASE COUNT ON ME ALWAYS."

What was this? A case of mistaken identity? What does he know about me?

Several cell phone calls yielded only a voice mail, no live response. I tried again the following day with the same lack of response, so I decided to continue the e-mail connection. Late in the evening, I wrote to thank Rivero Lake for his earlier e-mails and explained that I had rung his phone with no success.

I then made explicit my interest in the Codex Cardona, saying that I'd seen it twenty years ago, followed its trajectory up to its disappearance in New York, and then had seen the Internet posting in which he figured. I acknowledged that it might be asking a lot, but I would very much appreciate his version of the events if he felt comfortable giving them, and also if he might help me pick up the codex's trail again. I explained that I was writing an account of the Cardona and was interested in the academic and intellectual value of the document and took no side in the legal tangles and controversies. I would understand if he preferred to say nothing.

I knew I wouldn't have been so direct in a personal conversation, but it didn't seem that I was going to have one. And I needed the find the codex; I thought then that I couldn't solve the main mysteries without a corpus delicti.

The next morning I received a curt reply.

"TALK TO THE OWNER! HE'S THE PROPRIETOR!"

Isn't an "owner" the same as a "proprietor," I wondered? And which owner was Rivero Lake talking about?

"Do you mean Guillermo Gutiérrez?" I wrote. "Is *he* still the owner? I understood from the Internet posting that he had lost the Cardona."

"I KNOW NOTHING IN THIS REGARD. HE MUST BE THE OWNER!"

Understandably enough, Rivero Lake was not going to say anything about "his version of the events," but there appeared on my screen another abrupt and curious message:

"THE PIECE IS, AS YOU KNOW, IN THE HANDS OF A MADRID ANTIQUARIAN DEALER TO WHOM THE PROPRIETOR OWES MONEY. THE *ANTICUARIO* IS HOLDING THE PIECE TO GUARANTEE PAYMENT. THIS IS A PROBLEM BETWEEN THE TWO OF THEM."

How could he think that I might know this? Did he think that Gutiérrez Esquivel knew who held the codex? And that he might have told me? I ignored the "as you know" clause and wrote, "Can you most kindly tell me the name of the Madrid *anticuario*?"

"I DON'T KNOW. GOOD LUCK!"

And good night, Rivero Lake must have thought. Enough of this meddlesome gringo.[7]

What now? I'd come to a garden of forking paths, all leading into obscure and tangled woods with only faint blazes to go by. Two possibilities in Spain probably shouldn't be ruled out: the Catalan *hotelero* and the Madrileño *anticuario*. The codex could well be in Spain: Guillermo Gutiérrez Esquivel was an enthusiastic collector of Castilian artifacts and consequently had connections with antiquarian dealers in Madrid. Then too, Saorín Box, a man involved in the codex's disappearance in New York, was a Spaniard with connections to the arts and antiquities culture in Spain. The codex was originally represented, during its first appearance at Sotheby's in 1982, as being owned by a London resident "of Hispanic descent"; and there was the story that the Cardona had originally been in the possession of the Blanco White family in Seville for two centuries before it was put on the market. And now I had the direct, unequivocal statement from Rivero Lake (who should know) that the codex *is* in the hands of a Madrid antiquarian dealer, even if the dealer can't be named.

None of this information constitutes hard evidence, to say the least. It's unlikely, however, that the Cardona is in Mexico. Gutiérrez Esquivel has his antennae out but apparently hasn't picked up any signal of the codex's presence in his own country. It doesn't make sense that the dealers, after the collapse of the negotiations with Christie's in 1999, would bring the codex back to Mexico. There's always a risk carrying such obvious objects of national patrimony across international boundaries and having to deal with unpredictable customs officials.

The codex could still be in New York, but the rejection by Christie's would likely spook other prospective dealers there. Or perhaps it's been acquired by someone in a country other than Spain, in France or Russia or Japan. The Cardona could be anywhere on the planet.

Still, Spain seemed the most likely destination for the codex, and I felt that despite all the misleadings, misdirections, misconstructions, misconduct, lies, and subterfuge, it might still be possible to close in on the object of my quest. But whether there was any point in actually going to Spain to launch myself into what might easily turn into another wild-goose chase was another question. Where would I begin without any firm leads? What if I had a name but couldn't find the person? And even if I did, suppose he wouldn't even *see* me? What should I expect? That a complete stranger would ask me up to his room, offer me a drink, and bring out an exotic Mexican codex that he just happens to have lying around? I had to think about this whole business a bit more, to try to *imagine* the kind of person who might spend several million dollars for the Codex Cardona. A Mexican codex isn't everyone's cup of tea.

I planned to meet David for lunch in San Francisco and then a walk in the Presidio, bringing him up to date on the recent events in Mexico and the new leads and information I'd obtained there.

CHAPTER SEVENTEEN

Ibiza

"Look here, Sancho," said don Quixote, "I swear thou hast the
most limited understanding of any squire in the world. . . . Thus
what seems to thee a barber's basin seems to me Mambrino's
helmet and to another it will seem something else."

MIGUEL DE CERVANTES, *Don Quixote*

 David and I had just begun our walk in San Francisco's Presidio when the subject of following the Cardona's tracks to
Spain came up. We tried to imagine just how it might have
gotten from Christie's into the hands of the owner of a hotel
chain in Barcelona. David began in his enthusiastic, hortatory mode: I simply *had* to go to Barcelona. I could scout out the names of the main collectors of colonial documents and the principal antiquarians. There would be
no more than two dozen, say, who would deal in an expensive piece like the
Cardona, and if they themselves hadn't seen it, they would likely have leads.
Or, David continued, you could do some research on the Internet, find the
names of the great hotels and their corporate owners. Spend a few days
in Barcelona. "You might as well get around as long as you can," he said.
"What are you saving it for?"

As we went round and round with these ideas, a better notion occurred
to me. Why shouldn't David, who talks such a good game, go in place of
me? Of course, it was my project, but David had been closely involved from
the beginning. He knows Barcelona much better than I do—he spent six
months on sabbatical there a few years back—and he was currently at loose
ends. We'd split the cost and he'd be able to do the legwork.

We walked down from the eucalyptus grove to the parade ground. David
was warming to the possibility of his going to Spain, but the truth was
that both of us doubted the utility of a trip to Barcelona without thinking

through, or trying to imagine, a potential buyer of the codex and how to find him. Obviously there were many possible scenarios. What to do? To go or not to go, that was the question.

Iberia has a nonstop flight from San Francisco to Barcelona. David finds an inexpensive hostería a few blocks from La Rambla and sleeps off his jet lag. The next day, at the desk of the hotel Rey Juan Carlos I, he inquires after Gabriel Castells, the name, along with the name of the hotel, that had been mentioned in Mexico. A formal clerk whose badge reads—in English—"Assistant Manager" looks up from his ledger.

"May I ask who wishes to see Mr. Castells?"

David explains that he's a retired history professor who is most interested in old Mexican documents and books and had been told by a well-known rare book dealer in Mexico that Mr. Castells had a similar interest. The assistant manager casts him a skeptical glance and motions him on. "Mr. Castells's suite occupies much of the fourteenth floor. I'd start there, if I were you. Take those elevators, left out the door, and look for Fundación Ebusus."

Inside the suite, it's all glass and marble with a breathtaking panorama of Barcelona's ancient harbor laid out below. David briefly explains his presence to the receptionist—the name on the desk says Nuria Alsina—and asks formally for señor Gabriel Castells.

"Let me see," señora Alsina says, scrolling down a list on her computer screen. "Perhaps an assistant, señor Escarrer, can see you; it seems that's the area you're interested in." After a short wait, David is escorted into Escarrer's office. David explains once again that he's a professor from the United States interested in old documents and books and has come to Barcelona to see Gabriel Castells on the recommendation of a Mexican acquaintance whose name he'd be pleased to provide. Here he takes what must seem to anyone a curious leap, saying that he's heard of a Mexican codex, that he's been interested in it for some time, and that he's been told that it had been sold to an important hotel man in Spain.

Escarrer is no doubt baffled by this unanticipated and hardly logical explanation but takes note that the visitor has come a long way and is, after all, a professor, which commands more respect in Spain than in California. But what in the world am I doing? David thinks, sitting in this luminous office fourteen floors above the city of Barcelona, spinning out some idiotic fantasy for my friend back in California, which is somehow meant to connect the Codex Cardona to what seemed to be a kind of benevolent and extremely well-funded foundation. A probably disreputable former Mossad agent is the only link to Gabriel Castells, who is apparently the president of the Fundación Ebusus, since his name appears on a bronze plaque at the entrance to the suite.

Escarrer is courteous. "Mr. Castells is not in Barcelona at this time. We can ask his secretary if there might be space for you, a few days from now, perhaps on Tuesday; he plans to return then."

This is not going to work, David thinks. The hostería isn't cheap (seventy euros with breakfast), and his credit card must be close to the limit. But he waits. When he comes back to the hostería from coffee on Wednesday morning there is a message from señora Alsina saying that Mr. Castells will be able to see him the next day at 11:00.

Gabriel Castells is in his fifties, well taken care of, tailored, manicured, self-possessed. The room, really an elegant salon adjoining his office, has pieces on pedestals that David recognizes, from that museum in the Maria Luísa Park in Seville, as Visigothic. There's a large sixteenth-century map of Barcelona by Anton van den Wyngaerde (could it be the original?) and several other objets of understated luxury. David explains again his presence in Barcelona, which he thinks must seem unconvincing to Castells.

"And what makes you think," Castells asks in a cool, though not unfriendly, tone, "that I would be able to help in a search for a lost Mexican Codex?"

David plays the only card he has, producing the former Mossad agent's name, "whom I believe you know—he gave my partner your name in Mexico City two weeks ago, saying that perhaps you could help." David tries to lighten up the suddenly tense conversation by saying that perhaps his being here in Barcelona now shows a measure of desperation.

"That gentleman," Castells says after a long pause and an equally long look at David, "helped out the foundation in some business dealings six or seven years ago, and we stay in touch."

Castells rises; time is running out. Has David come all this way for nothing?

"Just let me say one other thing," David says. "I'm not in the antiquities trade, I have no interest in whatever legal issues there may or may not have been over the Mexican codex; I simply want to see it again. Another professor friend and I have had a scholarly involvement with this thing for over twenty years. I'll probably not get back to Barcelona."

This mawkish appeal to sentiment seems to have no effect, but David plows on: "So if there is any way, any clue, any suggestion, that you might have about the Mexican codex, I'd be grateful. I don't know what Franz Friedmann, our mutual acquaintance, had in mind, but he did give the impression that you might help me out."

Castells pauses, apparently intrigued.

"I'll tell you what. I will look into your question; it seems it's really your obsession. I think a person in our parent company"—Castells's English is really very good—"might be interesting to you. But you'll have to go to Ibiza. And I won't be able to get approval for three or four days. We have your phone number; my staff will try to get something for you."

"By the way," Castells adds with a thin smile, "the parent company is a hotel chain."

For the next three days, David manages to reread Orwell's *Homage to Catalonia* and keeps up with the daily *Herald Tribune* and *Le Monde*. Reading Orwell, sitting on a bench in the great walkway of La Rambla, the scene of tumultuous political demonstrations during the Spanish civil war, calls up mixed emotions. Orwell was much admired but also a stern critic of the communists, and David, a red-diaper baby from a family of patriotic American communists, knew two survivors of the Abraham Lincoln Brigade who had fought in Spain with great bravery. He sits on one of the cast-iron benches along La Rambla looking down to the port, trying to imagine this broad, leafy boulevard in Orwell's day, when the Anarchists controlled Barcelona, politics were in disarray, and customers didn't tip in the bars and cafes. That was something, he thinks, that he could have gotten behind.

On the fourth day, Nuria Alsina leaves a message with the kind lady in the hostería—whom by now David has completely charmed—that he is to fly to Ibiza, find his way to the Hotel Fenicia Prestige in Santa Eularia des Riu (owned, it turns out, by the parent company), book a room, and on the following day someone will come for him.

The parent company's driver picks David up at the Fenicia Prestige at four o'clock. They drive along the coast from Santa Eularia, turn inland on a well-kept gravel road, pass through low hills of pine and cork oak to a substantial but plain entrance gate. Two uniformed men emerge from a guard caseta and wave the driver through. Behind the gate the road climbs steeply through native plantings to an ocher villa surrounded by broad terraces. The Mediterranean lies spread out below. The driver helps David out of the Mercedes; another man appears, takes his carry-on satchel, and accompanies him to the marble-floored foyer. An older man, perhaps in his early seventies, rather short, ample, smiling, and unprepossessing, is waiting on the terrace. He puts out his hand and introduces himself in Spanish. "My name is José María Font Ruis, *a sus órdenes*. It's always a pleasure to meet a historian, especially one from the United States."

The sun is sinking into the hills behind the villa, illuminating the water stretching to the east. Even here, on the far western edge, at this time of day, the Mediterranean is still Homer's wine-dark sea, a calm, vast, tideless lake.

Font Ruis invites David to sit on the terrace. "Would you like a whiskey? We have Scotch, or a fino? Or even a small glass of the Priorat? I like it as an aperitif—although no one else does."

David, who knows nothing about wines, makes a good choice with the Priorat, an unusually big and deep purple wine from down the coast and inland from Barcelona. Font Ruis asks him about the journey from California to Catalonia, about President Bush's intentions, David's opinion of the present generation of Spanish academics, and his own historical interests.

David hasn't imagined talking about these subjects with a businessman, let alone a wealthy hotelero, the owner of a vast chain. Font Ruis then turns to the way Spain and Latin America are taught in the United States. What is the most innovative research being carried out and by whom? What is David's opinion of present-day Spanish historians? David is taken aback. He hasn't ever had a conversation like this at the University of California; but he's able to tread water, recalling his graduate school years.

"My uncle," Font Ruis at last reveals, "worked with Jaime Vicens Vives, whom I'm sure you know, on that huge project *La historia de Espana y America*. I still think it's an impressive work, five volumes, well designed, one of the few that tries to integrate the history of Iberia and America over the four colonial centuries."

"I loved my uncle," Font Ruis continues. "I wanted to become a historian. In fact, I've written a few things, essays, that sort of thing, which, if you stay long enough, perhaps I could show you? But then I got into the hotel business just after Franco passed on. One thing led to the next, and here I am with an enterprise that just keeps growing, and as you can see, quite comfortable. It was never what I wanted to do; it's very tedious."

Fortuitously, one of David's teachers at Madison admired Vicens Vives and the French Annales school he was associated with, so that David is at least familiar with the work. He talks with Font Ruis about Vicens, about Spain and America, about other historians they're familiar with, until servants bring out torches and tapas, some manzanilla from San Lúcar, and then more courses and better wines. David has a simple palate out of high principle and isn't much of a wine drinker.

Around midnight, Font Ruis takes a last sip of *café exprés* and shakes out his napkin. "Castells says you're interested in some of my collections; or rather, in the codex that the foundation acquired a few years ago. In fact, I think we saved it from a gang of irresponsible bandits."

Could this actually be happening, David wonders, or is this one more twist, the final twist, in the Cardona story? Would he be sent back to Castells at the foundation in Barcelona only to find that the codex has vanished again?

"Yes," David says, in the most even voice he can muster, "I'd like to see the Codex Cardona."

"I can have it brought up to my study now, or we'd have more time and be more rested tomorrow."

"Now would be fine if you're up to it."

Inside, in Font Ruis's study, two servants enter carrying a polished wooden box. They lift the codex onto a heavy, well-lit table and stand aside. Font Ruis motions David to come forward, and they began carefully to leaf through the first folios.

"It's a beautiful thing," Font Ruis says, raising his arms in supplication in the presence of art, "and for me, moreover, it represents the joining of Spain and America, something I was fascinated by in Vicens Vives's history project. Since our foundation acquired it, I've tried to learn as much as I can about other codices. I'm told that it's one of the three or four great ones of the early sixteenth century."

David has seen the two dozen or so slides that the Stanford people had snapped, the five color shots reproduced on Van Rijn's website, and a few from the set El Arquitecto had handed over to Andrés; but here is the whole enchilada, the amate-paper original with over four hundred pages, three hundred illustrations, the same rustic binding. Font Ruis pulls the great map of Mexico-Tenochtitlán from the box and opens out its folios.

"This is the prize," he says, "a treasure by itself. I've seen the Santa Cruz map in Uppsala, but this is the best. Perhaps you noticed at the foundation that we had the original Van den Wyngaerde map of Barcelona, a near contemporary of this one in the Codex Cardona. In a few years, when we finish the museum in Santa Eularia—a small museum with just a few, but exquisite, items devoted to the early cultural marriage of Spain and America—we'll have these two side by side. I'm sure you'd feel the same incredible pleasure that I do in touching or running your fingers over one of the many Roman and Phoenician pieces we have on this island, imagining the craftsmen fashioning such objects, their dreams and doubts. But in this case, I feel even more emotion, seeing in my mind's eye the master painters and Aztec scribes illustrating this codex, explaining their vanquished culture, something we know less well than we do that of the Greeks or Hittites."

David can't help feeling pleased that the codex is here rather than being lugged around Europe and the United States in a fiberboard suitcase by dubious dealers. One day it will surely be on display and available for scholarly examination. But, of course, he also knows that it should never have been removed from Mexico, from the people who had produced it in the first place. Still, it seems ungracious to say so, seeing Font Ruis's enthusiasm and knowing, at least, that the Cardona is in safe hands. Should he mention the question of provenance or the many recent laws governing national patrimony?

Font Ruis seems to sense David's inner conflict.

"When the codex was offered to us, Gabriel—Gabriel Castells—and I were assured that although it was obviously made in Mexico, it had been in the possession of a respectable Spanish family for centuries. Of course, one never knows for sure about these things. There was, in fact, some question about ownership; but a competent, experienced person—the man you heard about in Mexico—worked with us until we got to the bottom of the matter and he managed to obtain a clear title. Since you've been interested in the codex for so many years, you must know all of this. I fear I'm boring you with details."

"In any case," Font Ruis continues, "if you think about it, the Codex Cardona is as much a Spanish as a Mexican artifact. If it hadn't been for Capitan Cardona and Viceroy Mendoza and, say, the native painters and scribes with the Spanish friar Olmos in Tlatelolco looking over their shoulders, they would never have produced this work. Isn't that true?"

Not exactly, David thinks. Mexican *tlahcuilos* had been doing it for centuries. They were the indispensable artists and scribes necessary to produce the codex. The Spanish captain and the good friar, men whom Font Ruis mentioned as responsible for the Cardona, didn't have a clue, couldn't have produced this work. Font Ruis and David talk on into las altas horas de la mañana, two men in love with the history of America and Spain.

The next morning, David rises early and joins Font Ruis on the terrace for mangoes and a kind of Catalan zucchini bread and coffee. The summer sun climbs over the Mediterranean, and the jasmine shade is welcome. There is no way David can adequately express his thanks. Yesterday had been a day of days— brought on, David has to admit, by extraordinary luck—and what might seem, if one were to read about it, implausible coincidence. Nonetheless, side by side with the remarkable elephant folios in Font Ruis's library, there is still, on the terrace where they now sit together, the larger elephant of possible fraud, not yet mentioned in their long discussions. David feels he has to bring it up, ungracious or not. He pushes his chair back, the legs scraping across the tiled floor.

"You know, of course, José María,"—by now they are using the *tu* form—"that the Codex Cardona may not be real, I mean not an authentic sixteenth-century work."

Font Ruis's reaction stops David in his tracks.

"Collectors often face questions about authenticity, and maybe in some narrow sense the Codex Cardona is not 'real.' For me it is real. Or as don Quixote might have put it, the Cardona is as I would have it be. Some small-spirited souls may think that castles are really rustic inns or that Mambrino's golden helmet is only a barber's wash basin, or that Dulcinea is 'in reality' only Aldonza Lorenzo, and that don Quixote is mad to see them otherwise. I'm not mad, but I can clearly see that the Codex Cardona is a beautiful work that brings to life a lost world. It's a treasure. We all long for a sense of purpose and beauty. Why lose oneself in a tedious and shallow notion of the truth?"

David had read Cervantes's masterwork during a summer in London while doing some research in the British Museum, and he remembers now that most of don Quixote's good intentions, in fact, did only harm. But maybe there is another truth. Does it matter if this codex were produced out of hearsay, oral tradition, and garbled translations in an Aztec *tlahcuiloyan* in the 1540s, or by survivors of that culture half a millennium later, by modern *tlahcuilos* in a Mexico City workshop under brilliant, if fraudulent, guidance? In both cases, despite conquest, colonialism, imperialism, revolution, and now the devastation wrought by global capitalism, we can still see the long endurance, the persistence of the deeper features, of a still vital culture.

David doesn't try to lay these overwrought pensées onto Font Ruis's romantic mind, but he has to admit that his line about the search for "a tedious and shallow notion of the truth" is disquieting.

David and I had fallen into this fantasy while walking through the Presidio in San Francisco, and now we'd ended up, a little out of breath, at Fort Point, under the dramatic arch of the Golden Gate Bridge. We leaned against the rusty railing looking down at the starfish that seemed to be hanging on for dear life as the surf crashed against the rocks.

"Well, that's a pretty good story," I said, "a little far-fetched, but a lot of things in there could have happened; I mean, we did hear rumors from both the book dealer and El Arquitecto that the codex had been sold to a Spanish *hotelero*. I'm not claiming, of course, that our invented character José María Font Ruis acquired the Cardona, but you can imagine someone like that—lots of money, scholarly interests, and so on—being interested."

"Yes," David said, "and any new respectable owner, having doubts about authenticity, would go to some length, or have his subordinates make the efforts, to obtain documentation, however dubious. Obviously there are people—cultivated people, genuinely interested in history—people like our José María out there who may have acquired the Cardona. They don't have to be shady or unscrupulous characters the way we've sometimes imagined them."

"Of course not. And it's also hard to imagine that we'd actually ever find people like, say, an Escarrer or a Castells, who would listen to us instead of throwing us out on our ear; or that any new owner would actually be interested in Vicens Vives!"

"Not someone *exactly* like Font Ruis," David said, "but perhaps someone a bit like that. The point is that you have to follow the leads; you have to at least think of plausible possibilities."

"The don Quixote angle *is* a bit recherché; not to say over the top."

"What do you mean?" David said with a smile. "Your entire quest to find the Codex Cardona is nothing if not quixotic."

CHAPTER EIGHTEEN

A Madrid Anticuario

Oh, what a tangled web we weave,
When first we practice to deceive!

SIR WALTER SCOTT, *Marmion*

 I was reluctant to give up the possibility that some kind of Barcelona *hotelero* might be the current owner of the codex. Although the leads never rose above the level of hearsay, at least we have *converging* rumors from two independent sources that a "Spanish hotel man" was involved in the Cardona transaction. So speculation was not entirely implausible. Consequently the possibility of actually tracking down the present owner of the Cardona still wafted through my head. Besides, without actually being able to lay hands on the codex and leaf through its *amate* folios once again, this story would have no proper conclusion for the reader (or the writer).

There are things in this story we don't know, but many others we do. Let's leave behind the question of provenance, where the codex came from—whether the native village of Milpa Alta, a Sevillian manor house, or the imaginative pen and brush of a twentieth-century *erudito* such as Robert Barlow—and concentrate on where the book might be now. The story of the Cardona's brief time in the public view begins in mid-1998, continues through the months when Gutiérrez Esquivel presumably handed over the codex and the two oversized folio maps to the brothers Rivero Lake in Mexico City in October 1998, and ends in May 1999, when Christie's refused to take the codex on consignment. After that decision, now over nine years ago, the Cardona hasn't been heard of or seen publicly.

We know that as the summer of 1998 wore on, Gutiérrez Esquivel was desperate to find a buyer for his codex. We know he was in dire financial straits. His wife had suffered a stroke, and his son had cancer. I know the story of the wife is true because on the day Andrés Reséndez and I visited Gutiérrez Esquivel's studio, I opened the wrong door on the way to the bathroom and saw his immobilized wife stretched out on a narrow bed. Ignacio Bernal, who thought El Arquitecto might even have lost his house up in Las Lomas, corroborated his financial problems. For these reasons, Gutiérrez Esquivel agreed to accept the offer of Pedro Saorín Box, a Spanish artist and rare book and antiquities dealer, to unload the Cardona at a price much lower than previously anticipated. Also, according to El Arquitecto, Rodrigo Rivero Lake was enlisted—and promised payment—to provide advice and "security." Velia Meade, a third member of the sales team, signed an informal receipt for the codex on August 3, 1998.

We don't know who carried the codex to New York or who was actually involved in the negotiations with Christie's. Christopher Coover, now a prominent official in that institution, understandably wouldn't tell me whom he dealt with—but he did agree to tell me who was *not* present. According to Coover, after I rattled off their names, neither Rivero Lake, nor Velia Meade, nor Saorín Box was involved. This apparently means that the three people Gutiérrez Esquivel dispatched to New York to sell his codex did not reveal themselves to Christie's. Don Guillermo nevertheless thought that all three were in New York and "in collusion."

For his part, Gutiérrez Esquivel apparently *didn't even know* that the codex had been offered to Christie's. He exhibited no interest in Andrés's and my discussion about those negotiations when we talked with him in his studio. He claimed only to know that his envoys, maybe one, maybe two or three, had left Mexico with the codex and with instructions—disingenuous, to be sure—"to sell the piece only to a Mexican because of regulations governing national patrimony." Gutiérrez Esquivel, even eight years after the collapse of the sale in New York, still seems not to know what happened there. I received an e-mail on September 22, 2007, from Gutiérrez Esquivel's close friend, the distinguished clinical psychologist Anameli Monroy de Velasco, who wrote to me (in Spanish), "We know that Rivero Lake stole the codex from El Arquitecto but we don't know for sure to whom he sold it. We heard that it was sold to a Spanish *hotelero* but we know nothing more."

As for Rivero Lake, we know he was in New York, not only because Gutiérrez Esquivel describes in his Internet posting the meeting with him at the Plaza Hotel but also because Rivero Lake himself confirms this meeting.

But Rivero Lake says he was never involved at Christie's and moreover was never paid a cent for "all the effort I made with the paperwork." In fact, all three of El Arquitecto's presumed agents, Rivero Lake, Saorín Box, and Velia Meade, come and go like moving shadow-shapes. And somewhere along the line, Meade disappears.

Things obviously went awry in New York. Coover told me that the Cardona's "murky history" ultimately killed the negotiations with Christie's. He did give me the name of one "John Gloine" as "someone I might consult"; but as we've seen, I was unable to find such a person. Perhaps "Gloine" was a pseudonym. I thought for some time that this person might actually be Franz Friedmann, the "anonymous dealer" who told Ignacio Bernal that he'd been involved in the Christie's transaction. Gutiérrez Esquivel describes Friedmann as "another of Rivero Lake's *rufianes*"; his participation now seems unlikely.

Whoever was involved in the New York imbroglio—and we can't know unless this whole business is eventually ventilated in court—the friendship, or at least the business association, between Gutiérrez Esquivel and Rivero Lake deteriorated rapidly after the unraveling at Christie's. Both men returned to Mexico City, and shortly thereafter there occurred the distinctly unfriendly encounter in Rivero Lake's penthouse. We have two different accounts of this event: one, in Gutiérrez Esquivel's Internet posting, describes an angry scuffle after Rivero Lake tells El Arquitecto, referring to the codex, "I can't give it to you"; and Rivero Lake's account in an e-mail to me on September 15, 2008, in which he claims that Gutiérrez Esquivel appeared at his doorstep with lawyers and even threatened to unleash a pair of "gatilleros narcos" (narco gunmen) on him. Rivero Lake goes on to say in the same e-mail that "in 1999, I never had [the codex] in my hands" (nunca lo tuve en la mano). "The truth is that Pedro Saorín is the person who has the codex. Get in touch with him, he's holding it against money owed to him for debts accrued by El Arquitecto." This, as we've seen, repeats Rivero Lake's opinion e-mailed to me in September 2006; this time, however, he names the "Madrid antiquarian" dealer. Of course, this comment is in direct conflict with Gutiérrez Esquivel's often repeated statement that he knows only that Rivero Lake stole his codex and has no idea who has it now. Surely, if a Madrid antiquarian dealer wants payment for past debts incurred by El Arquitecto, El Arquitecto would know about it!

Meanwhile, back in New York, after Coover finally decided to turn down the Cardona, who would have picked up the newly wrapped codex from

Christie's in midtown Manhattan that spring day in 1999? Put another way, how did Gutiérrez Esquivel, expecting to receive several million dollars from the sale, end up holding an empty sack? We can imagine an edgy and even panicky meeting between Rivero Lake, Saorín Box, and maybe Velia Meade or "John Gloine" as they wondered where to go next. Were there other private collectors in New York who might be interested? Buyers in other countries? What about Japan? Or the Saudis? Or—what would seem the obvious question—should they not have returned the codex to its owner in Mexico City?

But then, perhaps the very absence of documentation that had spooked Christie's (and other previous buyers) now appeared as temptation. Neither Rivero Lake nor Saorín Box had signed receipts, a custom that El Arquitecto had explained "in some cases prevails in transactions in Mexico." In fact, the two men knew, there was no paper trail, no proof at all, of the Cardona's very existence.

However, it was also likely that Saorín Box, and presumably Rivero Lake as well, had incurred expenses during the long negotiations in New York. And, we recall, they'd received no monetary advance; their recompense, including Rivero Lake's $50,000 for "security," was to come from the proceeds of the sale. So, far from receiving the profit in excess of the $1.8 million that El Arquitecto had agreed to accept, Rivero Lake and Saorín Box were also left high and dry after the codex was rejected by Christie's.

Let us imagine, then, following Rivero Lake's allegation, that Saorín Box proposes that he take the codex to Madrid. He's a successful artist, deals in antiquities, is well connected to Spanish dealers. Moreover, it's reasonable to suppose that he and Gutiérrez Esquivel had previously worked together, collecting and selling art and antiquities. In fact, that day in his studio, we saw many such items; and Rivero Lake described El Arquitecto's collection in the hacienda Chiconcuac as "a marvelous thing." So it's not unlikely, given his financial straits, that Gutiérrez Esquivel may well have owed Saorín Box for past transactions and consequently, as Rivero Lake pointed out in the September 2006 e-mails, if the debt were paid, the codex would be returned: "this is a matter between the two of them." But this, of course, makes no sense, because in this case, if there were negotiations, El Arquitecto would surely know who has his codex and would not protest that he doesn't.

Anyway, case closed. In this scenario, Rivero Lake is exonerated; Saorín Box has a valuable piece probably worth more than the debts owed him by

El Arquitecto; the now invisible Ms. Meade seems not to complain; everyone gets something except Gutiérrez Esquivel, and he doesn't even know who stole the codex.

But wait: if Saorín Box only wants Gutiérrez Esquivel to reimburse him for debts and costs accrued in the negotiations with Christie's, why doesn't don Guillermo do so and retrieve his codex? Are the costs too high, out of his reach? If Saorín has put in a claim to him, why does Gutiérrez Esquivel not know that Saorín Box has the codex? It doesn't make sense. Then, too, why would Rivero Lake, with apparently nothing to gain, choose to out Saorín Box, his erstwhile accomplice, by revealing that Saorín actually has the Cardona in his possession? Finally, it may well be that Rivero Lake's latest information is out of date and Saorín Box has sold, and no longer has, the codex. Nine years is a long time to wait for Gutiérrez Esquivel to pay off his debts.

But then, we must ask, to whom might Saorín Box have sold the codex? Well . . . maybe to a Spanish *hotelero* with a villa in Ibiza!

How can we get at what is real or true in this story? To begin with, the entire business is complicated by the issue of cultural patrimony. The codex is "hot," and carrying it across international borders, let alone selling it, presents legal questions. That also means there are powerful incentives for the various people who have acquired, handled, and tried to sell the Codex Cardona, or currently to possess it, not to come clean—and painful penalties if they do—because it was illegally acquired and unlawfully marketed. No doubt Saorín Box, or anyone else involved in the trade, is keenly aware of these facts.

Here, of course, I have once more entered the realm of speculation in the midst of unknowable things. What we do know is that a Mexican painted book known as the Codex Cardona once existed and has now disappeared. There is strong evidence from expert evaluation that it is an extraordinary, even unique, artifact of high historical and cultural value that was hidden away, presumably, for some four hundred and fifty years. "Presumably," because the date of its creation has never been definitively established. Embedded in the story of the Codex Cardona are all kinds of distortions, false trails, allegations, and speculations regarding its antecedents, authenticity, and present location. Will the Codex Cardona, in its integral form, ever be seen again? That's something else we don't know.

CHAPTER NINETEEN

Resolution

Old men ought to be explorers.

T. S. ELIOT, "East Coker"

 During our visit to his studio, Gutiérrez Esquivel had rue-fully shaken his head, fearing that whoever has the Codex Cardona now may not appreciate its importance — not com-prehend that it's a major Mexican cultural treasure. He has always insisted that *he* was the person who first recognized the coherence of the sixteenth-century papers scattered on Enrique Medina's floor, res-cuing the codex from breakup into scattered folios. It was sad to imagine, don Guillermo said, but possible to think, that some uncultured soul might now put this treasure on the back shelf in the modern equivalent of a musty, private Sevillian library, where it would rest for another 450 years: all those exotic paintings made by those Mexica *tlahcuilos* nearly five centuries ago, lost forever.

When I thought about it, it was also possible that the present owner — I should say "possessor" — of the Cardona would know very little, if any-thing, about the controversy over its authenticity. He or she might not have the slightest notion of the rumors that it may once have been among Felipe Neve's possessions on the eighteenth-century Mexican frontier; or may once have been held by José María Blanco White and Baron Schultzenberg-León; or may recently have been found by excavators in the subfloor of the Hospital de Betlemitas in what once was Mexico-Tenochtitlán; or even might have been falsified by Robert Barlow's *tlahcuilos* as a labor of love in the 1940s. It's unlikely that the present owner will know about Enrique

Medina's antiquities gallery or the Indian community at Milpa Alta. Any documentation accompanying the codex today is unlikely to report all this shady background.

Michel van Rijn's web pages dealing with the Cardona have been taken down. There will be no explanatory packet of documentation tucked into the codex's carrying case as there was at Sotheby's and the Getty. Any present seller, worried about revealing incriminating secrets, would not include that baggage. Or far worse, I wryly mused, until the publication of this book becomes reality, the owner will never get to hear of an aging gringo professor who got his teeth into a quixotic search and couldn't let go.

After two decades of searching for the truth about the Codex Cardona, I'd come to the opinion that it probably *was* an authentic sixteenth-century work that probably *did* turn up in an Indian village in the Valley of Mexico in the twentieth century. But we can't be certain. For that we'd have to have the codex in hand (or rather, in several expert hands) to subject the text and illustrations to professional scrutiny—an effort the Stanford anthropologists thought would occupy a decade of their lives and one they were not prepared to make.

There are, of course, the hundreds of color slides that Andrés and I brought back from Gutiérrez Esquivel's studio to the University in California. Andrés had the entire collection digitized, and we returned the originals to don Guillermo. When we assembled the slides on the computer, however, it immediately became apparent that the order was all a jumble; worse, many, perhaps some of the best illustrations, were missing. Gutiérrez Esquivel had lent some boxes to less-than-scrupulous friends. A few other slides have simply disappeared; I suspect they were used in the Internet posting and then went astray. One of these was the exceptional painting of Cortés lifting a corner of the coffin of his wife, whom he had recently—probably—murdered. Enrique Medina, for his part, kept at least thirty folios.

I had my usual long Thursday afternoon coffee with Andrés and drove out to the house, lost in my frustration over the lack of a satisfying denouement to the Cardona mystery. I got out of the car, walked over to Alex's garden and sat down on a fragile bench. Alex had made flourish all kinds of plants. I could see now what she meant all those years ago when she said the house "had possibilities." She had tuberoses, native to Mexico, a Joseph's coat, and a giant Banksia rose. There were canna, not the ordinary kind but the exotic "Tropicana" variety with red, green, and yellow leaves; four-foot-tall clusters of rudbeckia, newly in bloom; scads of achillea, or yarrow; all kinds of salvia and frothy-flowered Russian sage. There were red hot pokers, coneflowers with spiky seedpods, lantana—you name it. Even clematis and a climbing plumbago. I'd been told the names of all these plants and forgotten them a hundred times. Finally she'd written them down, and I'd been able to memorize a few.

Alex was standing by the plumbago at the entrance to the garden, cooling off in the first breezes up from the bay. The Cécile Brunners she'd planted the day twenty-four years ago when I first saw the Cardona had spread over the trellis, but I noticed that the blossoms had dried, a reminder that "the flower that once has blown forever dies."[1]

She gave me a peck on the cheek. "How was your coffee with Andrés?"

"Well, we had a little talk about some hypothetical travels of the codex after it left Christie's. But we don't have any better idea of where it is than we had before. There are rumors and more false trails. Maybe I've come not to a garden of forking paths but to an end with no conclusion. It's like sailing for years on the sea without ever finding the whale."

The next day, sitting in my study and obsessively mulling over once again the tangled story of the Codex Cardona—all the lies and deception, the false trails laid out, the unscrupulous dealers—the most likely denouement to my quest suddenly became obvious.

It's *possible* that the codex may appear again, and if it does become public, the mystery will be solved and people will flock to read this book—well, not exactly *flock*, but there will be some interest. But it's been nine years since the codex was (apparently) stolen after its appearance at Christie's, and there's no clear sign of it anywhere: not on the Internet, in the rare book and manuscript catalogs, in newspapers, or in academic gossip. Rodrigo Rivero Lake's revelations are dramatic and plausible, but unconfirmed by physical evidence. There is no new word from El Arquitecto, from Ignacio Bernal, from the "Madrid *anticuario*," or even from someone like the Spanish *hotelero* David and I speculated about.

Much more likely—it's almost certain, given the circumstances—the person who has it now, understandably apprehensive about the problems of provenance and ownership, and aware of the risk of illegal trafficking in cultural patrimony, would do the logical thing: sell off the codex *piece by piece* starting with those spectacular illustrations and then the odd page of script. There are people who'd pay *something* for even a single sheet of sixteenth-century text on *amate*, not to mention the Mexico-Tenochtitlán map that both Gutiérrez Esquivel and Rivero Lake thought would alone sell for $1.5 million. You had to remember that the Cardona was not *bound*, like the Telleriano-Remensis and the Mendoza, but rather loose-leafed with cardboard covers tied with string—easy to dismember.

So it's very likely that there's *no longer in existence* a Codex Cardona, that its identity as a single, coherent sixteenth-century codex is destroyed. *It's gone*, cannibalized, tossed to the four winds, like Hemingway's big fish torn apart by the sharks. In fact, Enrique Medina, the dealer in the Pasaje de las Flores who picked out for himself some thirty pages, had already begun this pillage. Moreover, the 692 slides in the original collection that Stephen Colston used for the Getty evaluation have been ransacked by one of El Arquitecto's untrustworthy aides. We found that over a hundred slides—presumably several of the most valuable ones—are missing.

Then it dawned on me that the *only* record of the original Codex Cardona, the only place the entire, coherent work *actually exists*, is in this book!

It's not that I've sailed the seven seas without finding the whale: *I found it.* Described it. Told of its contents. Cited the experts on its value and beauty. And I have some scattered color slides—and that little corner of the *amate* folio that Schwarz tore off for me at the Crocker Lab. I had to remember that if it weren't for Melville there would be no Moby Dick; and without my book, no story of the lost codex. It's gone; no one will ever see the actual painted book that I first saw at the Crocker Lab.

I walked out from my study to the garden, where Alex was again watering her plants. She kept the hose running and turned to look at me.

"You look relieved. Did your codex finally turn up?"

"It's gone," I said, "I think forever. But there were a few things to be said about it."

NOTES

1 THE CROCKER LAB

1 Seaver, *Maps, Myths, and Men.*
2 See León-Portilla, *Códices*, for a summary of Mexican codices.
3 *El universo del amate*, 15.

2 A WORLD OF PAINTED BOOKS

1 *New Yorker*, December 17, 2007, 62.
2 Quiñones Keber, *Codex Telleriano-Remensis.* All subsequent quotations regarding this codex are taken from this work.
3 Nicholson, "History of the Codex Mendoza," 1–14.
4 Nuttall, "Standard or Head-Dress?"
5 Nicholson, "History of the Codex Mendoza," 2.
6 Quiñones Keber, *Codex Telleriano-Remensis*, 87.
7 Ricard, *The Spiritual Conquest of Mexico*, 34–38.
8 Schwaller, "Tracking the Sahagún Legacy."

4 SOTHEBY'S OF LONDON

1 Kagen, *Urban Images*, 51–64.
2 Rodrigo Rivero Lake, e-mail to the author, September 12, 2007.

5 THE GETTY

1 Wood, "The Techialoyan Codices."

9 SEVILLE AND THE FIRESTONE

1 Edwin Beilharz, *Felipe de Neve.* The information on Felipe de Neve's life and career is based on this book.

1 Ricard, *Spiritual Conquest of Mexico*, 38.
2 Calderon, *Life in Mexico*, 141.

13 AN INTERNET POSTING

1 "Challapampa, la historia de un altar que regresó," *Cultura* (Lima, Peru), February 6, 2006, 1–2, http://peru21.com.

16 THE HIGH END

1 McCosh, "Mexican Antiquario." See also the laudatory account in Reyes Fragoso, "Goza de un privilegiado olfato."
2 "Zona VIP," *El Universal On Line* (Mexico City), January 22, 2006, http://www.eluniversal.com.
3 *New York Times*, October 8, 2006. See also Cearley, "Painting Figures in a Museum Whodunit."
4 Notimex.com (Mexican News Agency), July 2004, http://www.notimex.com.
5 "Challampa, la historia de un altar que regresó."
6 *Cronaca: Past Imperfect, Present Subjunctive, Future Conditional* (an online compilation of news, archaeology, and history edited by David Nishimura), January 25, 2005, 1–2.
7 To my complete surprise, between September 12 and 19, 2008, I received a series of unanticipated e-mails from Rodrigo Rivero Lake. After our last and rather abrupt exchanges two years earlier, we'd had no further contact. "I've been thinking a lot about you," he wrote. "Tell me if you want me to clarify a few things. The confusion over the business with El Arquitecto hasn't been agreeable to me." Why, after such a long lapse, did Rivero Lake seek me out? I don't know. Whatever his motive, however, I was more than happy to take up his offer. The new information contained in this chapter, as well as in the previous accounts, comes from those e-mails. Copies of all e-mail communication are in my possession.

19 RESOLUTION

1 Fitzgerald, *The Rubáiyát of Omar Kayyám*, 76.

BIBLIOGRAPHY

ARCHIVES

Blanco White Family Papers. Firestone Library. Princeton University. Boxes 5, 15, 16, 17, 18, 19.

Archivo General de Indias, Seville. Leg. 1420, pp. 74ff. Will and Testament of Felipe de Neve y Padilla.

PERSONAL COMMUNICATIONS

The following are the principal people with whom I've had sustained and useful telephonic and e-mail exchanges and personal conversations between August 1986 and April 2008.

Ignacio Bernal (pseudonym), rare book and manuscript dealer, Mexico City, conversation, August 25–26, 2006.

Gordon Brotherston, visiting professor, Stanford University, conversation, September 2005.

Stephen Colston, professor, California State University, San Diego, e-mail exchanges, 2000–2003; conversation, May 14, 2007.

Christopher Coover, curator, Christie's of New York, telephone calls, July 2005 and February 2006.

Enrique Florescano, Mexico City, conversation, February 2005.

James Fox, professor, Anthropological Sciences, Stanford University, conversation, May 24, 2002, September 2005.

Guillermo Gutiérrez Esquivel, Mexico City, conversation, August 23, 2006.

Cecilia Lemberger, Mexico City, conversation, August 23, 2006.

Víctor Lomelí Delgado, Mexico City, conversation, August 2006.

Enrique Medina (pseudonym), antiquities dealer, Mexico City, conversation, August 26, 2006.

Anameli Monroy, Mexico City, e-mail exchanges, September 22, 2007.

Henry Nicholson, professor, UCLA, telephone conversation, January 2006.

Nicholas Olsberg, Getty Museum, telephone conversations, May and November 2005.

Jaime Ortíz Jafous, Mexico City, conversation, August 25, 2006.

Anthony Pagden, professor, UCLA, telephone conversation, May 1, 2006.

Rodrigo Rivero Lake, Mexico City, e-mail exchanges, August 2006, December 24, 2006, September 13–19, 2008.

Richard Schwab, University of California, Davis, conversations, 1986, 2006–7.

Thomas F. Schwarz, bookseller, Mill Valley, Calif., conversations, May 2006.

David Sweet, Santa Cruz, Calif., conversations, 1986–2009.

Wim de Wit, Getty Museum, e-mail exchanges, October 13, 2005, November 18, 2005.

Stephanie Wood, University of Oregon, e-mail exchanges, 2000–2001; Sonoma, Calif., conversation, May 2006.

PUBLISHED SOURCES

Beilharz, Edwin A. *Felipe de Neve: First Governor of California.* San Francisco: California Historical Society, 1971.

Berdan, Frances F., and Patricia Rieff Anawalt. *The Codex Mendoza.* 4 vols. Berkeley: University of California Press, 1992.

Boone, Elizabeth Hill. *Stories in Red and Black: Pictorial Histories of the Aztecs and Mixtecs.* Austin: University of Texas Press, 2000.

Calderon, Fanny. *Life in Mexico: The Letters of Fanny Calderon de la Barca.* Ed. and annotated by Howard T. Fisher and Marion Hall Fisher. Garden City, N.Y.: Doubleday, 1966.

Cearley, Anna. "Painting Figures in a Museum Whodunit." *San Diego Union-Tribune,* December 9, 2004.

"Challampa, la historia de un altar que regresó." *Cultura* (Lima, Peru), February 6, 2006. http://www.peru21.com.

Eliot, T. S. "East Coker." *Four Quartets.* New York: Harcourt, 1968.

Fitzgerald, Edward. *Rubáiyát of Omar Khayyám.* London: Penguin Books, 1989.

Gibson, Charles. *The Aztecs under Spanish Rule.* Stanford, Calif.: Stanford University Press, 1964.

Guaman Poma de Ayala, Felipe. *El primer nueva corónica y buen gobierno.* Ed. John V. Murra and Rolena Adorno. Mexico City: Siglo Veintiuno, 1980.

Handbook of Middle American Indians. Ed. Robert Wauchope. Austin: University of Texas Press, 1964–76.

Haude, Mary Elizabeth. "Identification and Classification of Colorants Used during Mexico's Early Colonial Period." *Book and Paper Group Annual* 16 (1997): 1–15.

Hazlitt, William. *Characteristics: In the Manner of Rochefoucault's Maxims. The Complete Works of William Hazlitt,* ed. P. P. Howe, vol. 9. London: Dent, 1932.

Kagen, Richard L. *Urban Images of the Hispanic World, 1493–1793.* New Haven, Conn.: Yale University Press, 2000.

Keen, Benjamin. *The Aztec Image in Western Thought*. New Brunswick, N.J.: Rutgers University Press, 1971.

King, Edward [Lord Kingsborough]. *Antiguedades de Mexico*. Mexico City: Secretaría de Hacienda y Crédito Público, 1964–65.

León-Portilla, Miguel. *Códices: Los antiguos libros del Nuevo Mundo*. Mexico City: Aguilar, 2003.

Lockhart, James. *The Nahuas after the Conquest*. Stanford, Calif.: Stanford University Press, 1992.

McCosh, Daniel I. "Mexican Antiquario." *Latin CEO: Executive Strategies for the Americas*, May 2001.

Mundy, Barbara E. *The Mapping of New Spain*. Chicago: University of Chicago Press, 1996.

Nicholson, H. B. "The History of the Codex Mendoza." In *The Codex Mendoza*, ed. Frances F. Berdan and Patricia Rieff Anawalt, vol. 1, 1–14. Berkeley: University of California Press, 1992.

Nuttall, Zelia. "Standard or Head-Dress?" *Archaeological and Ethnological Papers of the Peabody Museum* 1, no. 1 (1888).

Quiñones Keber, Eloise. *Codex Telleriano-Remensis: Ritual, Divination, and History in a Pictorial Aztec Manuscript*. Austin: University of Texas Press, 1995.

Randall, David A. *Dukedom Large Enough: Reminiscences of a Rare Book Dealer, 1929–1956*. New York: Random House, 1962.

Reyes Fragoso, Arturo. "Goza de un privilegiado olfato." *El Universal*, December 16, 2007.

Ricard, Robert. *The Spiritual Conquest of Mexico*. Trans. Leslie Byrd Simpson. Berkeley: University of California Press, 1966.

Robertson, Donald. *Mexican Manuscript Painting of the Early Colonial Period*. Norman: University of Oklahoma Press, 1994. Originally published by Yale University Press, 1959.

Schwaller, John Frederick. "Tracking the Sahagún Legacy: Manuscripts and Their Travels." In *Sahagún at 500: Essays on the Quincentenary of the Birth of Fr. Bernardino de Sahagún*. Berkeley: Publications of the Academy of American Franciscan History, 2003.

Scott, Walter. *Marmion*. 1808. London: BiblioBazaar, 2006.

Seaver, Kirsten A. *Maps, Myths, and Men: The Story of the Vinland Map*. Stanford, Calif.: Stanford University Press, 2004.

Simmons, George. "Patrimonio: Arte y hurto." *El Comercio* (Peru), September 17, 2006.

El universo del amate. Mexico City: Museo Nacional de Culturas Populares, 1982.

von Hagen, Victor Wolfgang. *The Aztec and Maya Papermakers*. New York: J. J. Augustin, 1944.

Wood, Stephanie. "The Techialoyan Codices." In *Sources and Methods for the Study of Postconquest Mesoamerican Ethnohistory*. Eugene: Wired Humanities Project, University of Oregon, 2007.

ARNOLD J. BAUER is a professor emeritus of history at the University of California, Davis. He is the author of *Goods, Power, History: Latin America's Material Culture* (2001) and *Chile y algo más: Estudios de historia latinoamericana* (2004).

Library of Congress Cataloging-in-Publication Data

Bauer, Arnold J.
The search for the Codex Cardona / Arnold J. Bauer.
p. cm.
"On the trail of a sixteenth-century Mexican treasure."
Includes bibliographical references and index.
ISBN 978-0-8223-4596-1 (cloth : alk. paper)
ISBN 978-0-8223-4614-2 (pbk. : alk. paper)
1. Codex Cardona.
2. Nahuas—Mexico—History—16th century.
3. Nahuas—Mexico—Manuscripts.
4. Manuscripts, Mexican.
I. Title
F1219.73.B38 2009
972'.01—dc22
2009030093